DIDEROT: THE VIRTUE OF A PHILOSOPHER

CAROL BLUM

Diderot: The Virtue of a Philosopher

THE VIKING PRESS / NEW YORK

To my husband, Martin,
this book is lovingly dedicated

Library of Congress Cataloging in Publication Data

Blum, Carol, 1934–
    Diderot: the virtue of a philosopher.

    Bibliography: p.
    1. Diderot, Denis, 1713–1784. I. Title.
B2016.B54   194 [B]   74-490
ISBN 0-670-27227-2

Note on Abbreviations

The sources from which I have quoted most frequently are abbreviated as follows:

A.-T. = Diderot, Denis. *Œuvres complètes.* J. Assézat and Maurice Tourneux, eds. 20 vols. Paris: Garnier Frères, 1875–77.

O.e. = Diderot, Denis. *Œuvres esthétiques.* Paul Vernière, ed. Paris: Garnier Frères, 1959.

O.p. = Diderot, Denis. *Œuvres philosophiques.* Paul Vernière, ed. Paris: Garnier Frères, 1956.

O.r. = Diderot, Denis. *Œuvres romanesques.* Henri Bénac, ed. Paris: Garnier Frères, 1959.

C. = Diderot, Denis. *Correspondance.* Georges Roth and Jean Varloot, eds. 16 vols. Paris: Editions de Minuit, 1955–70.

C.l. = Grimm, Melchior, and Diderot, Denis. *Correspondance littéraire philosophique et critique.* 16 vols. Paris: Longchamps, 1813.

D.S. = *Diderot Studies.* Vols. 1 and 2. Otis E. Fellows and Norman L. Torrey, eds. Syracuse: Syracuse University Press, 1949, 1952.

―――――, Vol 3. Otis E. Fellows and Gita May, eds. Geneva: Droz, 1961.

―――――, Vols. 4–7. Otis E. Fellows, ed. Geneva: Droz, 1963–65.

―――――, Vols. 8–15. Otis E. Fellows and Diana Guiragossian, eds. Geneva: Droz, 1966–72.

O.c. = Rousseau, Jean-Jacques. *Œuvres complètes.* Bernard Gagnebin, Robert Osmont, and Marcel Raymond, eds. 4 vols. Paris: Bibliothèque de la Pléiade, 1959–66.

Acknowledgments

A number of teachers, colleagues, and friends have contributed to the preparation of this book through their encouragement and suggestions.

My friend and colleague Frederick Brown deserves more gratitude than I can express for his continual interest in every aspect of this work. His perceptive comments on organization and his patient ministrations to stylistic deficiencies were invaluable.

Otis E. Fellows of Columbia University not only set an example of fine scholarship through his editorship of the *Diderot Studies* but has shown a gratifying kindly interest in my work through the years. I would like to thank Jean Rousset of the University of Geneva for providing the illumination and lucidity of his work as well as encouragement of my efforts. John N. Pappas of Fordham University, Frederick Crews of the University of California, and Anthony Rizzuto of the State University of New York at Stony Brook were kind enough to read this manuscript in various stages of preparation, and I am very grateful for their interest and suggestions. G. Norman Laidlaw, Ivan Schulman, and Mark Whitney, in their capacity as chairmen of my department, gave me the opportunity to organize the courses in which the ideas in this book were first tested in the context of classroom discussion.

A sabbatical leave from the State University of New York at Stony Brook afforded me the leisure to pursue this study. A Summer Fellowship from the State University of New York Research Foundation enabled me to utilize the resources of the Bibliothèque Nationale in Paris.

Elisabeth Sifton's editorial belief in the value of this work enabled me to bring it to its present form. Hélène Volat-Shapiro gave valuable assistance in assembling bibliographical materials. Gerhard Vasco, Stony Brook's Assistant Librarian and distinguished eighteenth-century scholar, was unfailing and expert in his help. Deborah Tax cheerfully cooperated in the preparation of the manuscript.

Finally, I am grateful to my husband, not only for his unerring capacity to see the shape of my arguments better than I could, but most especially for his unfailing understanding and support.

Portions of this book appeared, in different forms, in the *PMLA* (March 1973), the *Esprit créateur* (Fall 1969), and *Studies on Voltaire and the Eighteenth Century* (LXXXVII, 1972).

In translating French quotations into English, I have been here and there obliged to sacrifice stylistic considerations to insure the most accurate possible rendering of the original text.

Contents

DIDEROT: THE VIRTUE OF A PHILOSOPHER

1/Probity without Religion

A man's vision of the good—in himself, in the world around him, and in the productions of the human spirit—forms a unique and coherent structure, although its shape may not always be apparent beneath the wrappings imposed by an era or a temperament. When men are endowed with the prodigious energies of genius, like Denis Diderot and his friend Jean-Jacques Rousseau, the dimensions of the structure may be enlarged to a scale so imposing that it dominates the landscape of the human mind.

Both Diderot and Rousseau were driven by a powerful need to possess virtue, in the sense of intellectual mastery as well as personal worth. Rousseau's intuition of his own goodness and of the possibilities of goodness in society and art was born all of a piece, when, in 1749, on the way to visit Diderot in prison, he received the essential argument of his discourse on the arts and sciences like revelation. From that time until his death in 1778, the vision of the pure self, at odds with a corrupt and devitalizing society, manifested itself in myriad forms. His basic conceptions reflected the events of his troubled life, but ultimately Rousseau's writings can be read as a single saga—now lyrical, now prophetic, but always elaborating an immutable, consistent comprehension of the nature of good and evil. From the self-infatuated Narcissus of his first play to the desperate personage of his later years, convinced that he was the only human being left in a universe of automatons, Rousseau clung with perfect fidelity to the vision he saw on the road to the dungeon at Vincennes. Thus a scholar like Jean Starobinski was able to make a brilliantly convincing interpretation of Rousseau's thought [1] * by penetrating the disguises of Rousseau's various political, pedagogical, fictional, and self-revelatory writings to show the unchanging organization of thought lying directly beneath the surface.[2] Rousseau's construction is like the mist-shrouded castle of a mad king; its details, perceived one by one through the swirling fog reveal, in the end, an eccentric coherence.

The case of Diderot, Rousseau's most intimate companion and eventually worst enemy, is altogether different. His vision of virtue is more like a living thing, which developed and evolved in time, constantly striving to reconcile the demands of its inner nature with those of the world outside. To comprehend Diderot's attitudes toward the "good" man, or the "good" society, or the "good" work of art, we must see them as momentary compromises in a continuing struggle, rather than as glimpses of an ill-lit pristine whole. Yet, his thought possessed a unity as profound as Rousseau's. The two men were equally determined: one to incorporate the meaning of experience into a world view, the other to deny it.

In this study I have attempted to follow the meanings which the concept of virtue held for Diderot as they were expressed in his personal letters and his works. This may seem, in view of the sixteen volumes of his correspondence and the twenty volumes of works, to be a lengthy but straightforward task. Diderot's loquacity and apparent candor, however, often

---

* The superior figures refer to the Notes beginning on page 159.

served to mask his thought more effectively than reticence could. The difficulty in forming an adequate idea of his thought at any given moment stems from his deliberate use of the text as self-representation as well as vehicle for his arguments.

His works were intended to test an experimental image of the author upon the world and to explore a set of ideas. As his conception of himself evolved in reaction to the vicissitudes of his life, the picture he projected in his writings changed too, so that we perceive a self-portrait under constant revision. Behind Diderot's shifting personae, however—the author as skeptic in the *Pensées philosophiques,* as enthusiast in the *Eloge de Richardson,* as libertine in *Les Bijoux indiscrets,* or as sage in the *Entretien d'un père avec ses enfants*—one constant purpose is discernible. Diderot needed to experience himself as a virtuous man, and to be seen as a virtuous man by others. It was this preoccupation with virtue which led him to cast and recast the model of himself.

To us, living in the shell-shocked decades of a violent century, the word "virtue" has a quaint sound, recalling something that people thought about long ago and are now too sophisticated or too beleaguered to ponder any more. It carries overtones of still mustier concepts, like chastity, or charity, or obedience. It is hard for us to imagine the powerful and even dangerous ideas which the word, so bloodless to our ears, conveyed to a whole century. For Diderot, however, the need to be virtuous was felt as the one most urgent imperative of a passionate life; it directed the acts he performed and the words he wrote, from the time he entered the world of letters until he died. His obsession with virtue put him in the mainstream of pre-Revolutionary thought in France, although for him it was not merely a logical problem to be solved but rather the very core of being.

The eighteenth century, attempting to rid itself of the tyranny of superstition and irrationality, was a bit like a man who tried to pick a loose thread from his coat only to find he had unraveled the entire garment. To counter the burdensome oppression of the Church, which based its utilitarian argument upon the claim that only ecclesiastical authority in concert with the civil arm kept men from devouring one another, thinkers at the end of the seventeenth century had advanced the view that a society of atheists might theoretically be as virtuous as a society of Christians. Pierre Bayle, in his *Pensées sur la comète* of 1682, declared that humanity in general rarely allowed religious beliefs actually to influence conduct, making it apparent "that a society of atheists would practice civil and moral actions as well as other societies, provided that it punished crime severely and attached honor and disgrace to certain things." Nor should it be difficult to define these "certain things," for "there are ideas of honor among men which are the pure work of nature." [3]

Bayle had posed the question from the viewpoint of society alone, dismissing the issue of man's individual conscience in relationship to God. By 1734, Voltaire was going so far as to contend that man's only moral duty was to contribute to the preservation of order. Laws were necessary to a society "as rules are necessary in a game. Most of these laws seem arbitrary." The individual citizen, however, was bound to obey: "Virtue and vice, moral good and evil are in each country what is useful or harmful to the society." [4] Montesquieu took the argument a step further in the *Esprit des lois*. Not only did he show that society could influence its citizens to behave according to its will by the force of the laws and the example of the sovereign alone but he proposed that all religions, with the politic exception of the Catholic, be judged by a single criterion: the acceptable ones being those "that most conform to the good of society." [5]

In the eighteenth century, then, society had come to replace the Kingdom of God. As Robert Mauzi remarked, "never has man been conceived of less as a solitary being." [6] In the second half of the century the conviction was affirmed; to La Mettrie, Helvétius, and d'Holbach, the idea of virtue was indistinguishable from that of citizenship.[7] Venturing far beyond Bayle's tentative position that society *could* subsist without the threats of divine retribution imposed by religion, thinkers now propounded that the integrity of the social matrix itself, not the salvation of the individual, was the test by which human behavior was to be judged. The near unanimity this solution briefly enjoyed was not, however, to endure. Moving the center of man's gravity from Heaven to the City raised questions scarcely less complex than the scholastic conundrums of a previous era.[8]

Whether men joined together to form societies because, as Shaftesbury maintained, "only the social affections are capable of providing the creature with a real and constant happiness," [9] or whether they did so in defiance of nature, nobody could agree. For Rousseau, society was the antithesis of nature, the fall from a state of grace initiated by "the first one, who, having enclosed a plot of land, took it into his head to say: 'this is mine,' and found people simple enough to believe him." [10]

The Marquis de Sade and Robespierre both seized Rousseau's conception—that nature had made men good before they banded together to form societies—but each shepherded the idea to a different conclusion. Sade, the apologist for the pleasures of cruelty, saw natural man as the victim of social man, and "laws which are good for the society are very bad for the individuals who compose it." "Nature," he claimed, "the mother of us all, [gives us] the sacred exhortation to enjoy ourselves, at no matter whose expense." [11] For the dictator Robespierre, on the other hand, as he announced at the National Convention on February 7, 1794, shortly before he was himself guillotined by his fellow citizens, "fulfilling the wishes of nature" meant building a revolutionary society on two principles: "virtue, and its emanation, terror." [12]

To say that Diderot's thought was dominated by the problems of defining the words "nature," "society," and "virtue" is to understate the degree of his involvement. For Diderot, as for his friend and enemy Jean-Jacques Rousseau, these terms signified less a series of intellectual puzzles to be solved, than the key words in an ever-shifting definition of the self.[13]

"Virtue" was Diderot's mediation between the impersonal forces of nature and the superpersonal forces of society. His struggle to give adequate meaning to the word, on one hand, and to make that meaning consubstantial with his inner self, on the other, was the central movement of his life. This endeavor, as it was reflected in his works and his correspondence, is the subject of my study. I hope that in following Diderot's effort to reconcile the rational meanings attached to the word "virtue" with its emotional significance, we shall be able to comprehend more fully what the metaphors of a bygone age expressed, beneath an often archaic syntax, of universal human concern.

Diderot did not approach the world of letters from the avenue of aristocratic society, as did so many of the earlier generation of *philosophes.* Unlike Voltaire, who, as a youth, began by composing gallant verse to amuse his mistresses, or the Président de Montesquieu, already well established in the slightly debauched circles of the Regency when he turned his hand to writing, Diderot came to literature from a milieu whose values could scarcely have been more opposed to those of the *beau monde.*

His family in the Champagne town of Langres, where he was born in 1713, accepted two masters: religion and work. Elegance, refinement, and sophistication not only were remote from the goals of Didier Diderot, his wife, and their numerous children but would have been considered indecent affectations.[14] Diderot's father was a cutler by trade, specializing in the manufacture of surgical equipment, which, in those days, was often made to order for the individual physician. Before the advent of mass-produced cast-steel medical instruments, a surgeon carried his own specially made tools about with him. In some cases, such as that of the famous Drs. Chamberlen's forceps, they were wrapped so that the secrets of their design could not be guessed by inquisitive competitors. The fine reputation which Diderot's father apparently enjoyed in this exacting métier would place him in the upper ranks of the artisan class. When he was not at work in the shop adjoining their house, Diderot *père*, in his son's memory, led the life of a lay saint. "He was known throughout his province," Diderot wrote in 1771, "for his rigorous probity. He was more than once chosen as arbitrator between his fellow citizens, and strangers whom he did not know often confided the execution of their last wills and testaments to him. The poor mourned his loss when he died" (*O.p.*, 409).

The family seal bore the inscription: *"Virtus et labor patrum fasti,"* "The virtue and labor of the fathers bring happiness." [15] It may be said, however, that for the younger Diderot the motto brought a share of anguish as well. For all of Diderot's life his father loomed over him as an archetype of rectitude, the excellence of his blades commensurate with the integrity of his character. Like some awesome Old Testament patriarch, Diderot's father was to tower in his son's mind for many years, both as the model of correct behavior and as the menacing judge of failure.

Diderot had a younger brother, Didier-Pierre, with whom he enjoyed approximately the same warm fraternal relations that Cain shared with Abel. Denis was infinitely dear to his father, despite his innate rebelliousness and headstrong behavior, while Didier, meek as a lamb, embracing the familial piety to the point of becoming a priest, never succeeded in usurping his brother's place in their father's heart. Didier surpassed even his family in the scrupulosity of his religious observances, leading a life of piety in its narrowest sense, while Denis, off in Paris ostensibly studying theology himself, tasted the sweetness of *la vie de bohème*. Many years later, after Denis Diderot was an established spokesman for the scandalous freethinkers, he quoted his father as saying: "I have two sons. One is as devout as an angel; they say the other has no religion. I do not know why it is but I could not help loving the one with no religion better" (*C.*, II, 177).

Diderot made his way to Paris in 1728 or 1729, supposedly to prepare for an ecclesiastical career. Although evidence suggests that he attended either the Jesuit Collège Louis-le-Grand or the Jansenist Collège d'Harcourt, it was not long before he rejected the tranquil pleasures of theology in favor of those for which Paris was justly more celebrated: he began his pursuit of ideas that were not conventional and women who were not respectable. He appears to have made the best of both, and the connection between the two illicit indulgences was central to his personality: "My thoughts," he was to remark some years later in *Le Neveu de Rameau*, "are my harlots" (*O.r.*, 395).

Little is known in detail of Diderot's life in Paris between his arrival and his marriage in 1743, but from Arthur Wilson's excellent reconstruction of those shadowy years emerges a young man in intense pursuit of many pleasures, both spiritual and mundane. His abundant energies seem to have been all the more plentiful because they were directed to no particular purpose. His many courtships did not lead him into marriage, nor did his preprofessional studies lead him into any profession. Instead, he devoted more than a decade to an avid amateurism, reading law and theology, mastering mathematics, Latin, Greek, and English; visiting the theater; picking up odd jobs; and cadging what he could from his family.

From various autobiographical fragments and letters, a picture is assembled of the young Diderot as drifter, long exploiting his father's generosity but rejecting his tutelage. It was as if the adolescent disparity between the intellectual life and the private life were being artificially prolonged. Unwilling to accept his father's ambitions for him, Diderot seemed at the same time incapable of freeing himself from his domination altogether, remaining in part financially dependent upon his father while secretly defying him. His daughter, Mme de Vandeul, recalls in her memoirs the story of how Diderot pretended to a vocation as Carmelite monk, inducing one Frère Ange to advance him large sums of money. When Frère Ange demanded that his proselyte keep his end of the bargain, Diderot told him he was not interested and that he should go collect the money from Father Diderot in Langres.[16]

Looking back on this rebellious period of his youth some forty years later, the aging Diderot sympathized with the pain he must have caused his parents: "It is midnight. I am alone, I remember those good folk, those good parents; and my heart tightens when I think of all the anxieties thy must have experienced over the fate of a violent and impassioned young man, abandoned without guidance to an immense capital, the center of crime and vice. I made my father unhappy and my mother grieve as long as they lived" (*A.-T.*, XVII, 335).

If he was a disgrace by Langres's standards during those years in his corner of bohemian Paris, he was not the only young man causing tears to be shed in the provinces. Franco Venturi, in his study *La Jeunesse de Diderot,* describes the milieu of obscure writers, artists, and musicians drawn to Paris not only from all over France but from the rest of Europe, in which Diderot spent his days and his nights. The men with whom he dined at the Hôtel Panier Fleuri or played chess at the Café Royal ranged from eventually respectable types like Sartine, who was to be Chief of Police, or the future

Cardinal de Bernis, to unrepentant eccentrics such as the irascible pornographer Fougeret de Monbron, or Baculard d'Arnaud, imprisoned in the Bastille for composing a ballet called "The Art of Fucking." They were a colorful lot, and the many hours Diderot spent in their company left him with a great store of observations, anecdotes, and conversations upon which he was to draw time and time again in his works.

In 1742, as Diderot approached thirty, the year of his legal majority, he made up his mind to marry, a step which to some extent separated him from his Left Bank friends. Antoinette Champion and her mother ran a small linen shop in Paris. "She was as beautiful as an angel," Diderot later recalled, "and I wanted to go to bed with her" (*A.-T.*, XI, 265–66). But Antoinette was conventional and devout; her insistence on the proprieties forced Diderot to go back to Langres and tell his father of his matrimonial plans. He returned to his boyhood home in December 1742, but instead of immediately stating his intentions, he lapsed into a state of aimless dawdle, hanging about the house, apparently hoping his parents would guess what he had in mind without his having to put it into words.

In his letters to his betrothed from this period, Diderot sounds appalled by the step he was about to take and yet too afraid of Antoinette's wrath to withdraw his promise. One has the impression he chose his bride-to-be in part because she was a worthy opponent for his father, as strong-willed and implacably pious as the old cutler himself. It was as if only a new tyranny could deliver him from the old. However, in the family discussions of Diderot's future which preceded his declaration of intent to marry, it must be said that his father behaved with admirable constraint. He insisted only that his thirty-year-old son settle on some sort of career. "After a sermon two yards longer than usual," Diderot told Antoinette, "[my father] gave me full liberty to do as I please, provided that I do something" (*C.*, I, 29). But even that elastic proviso seemed too constricting; within a short time his father was reduced to assuring Diderot that he could remain in Langres "with full power to do nothing." It is curious to think of Diderot, soon to embark upon one of the most demanding and arduous tasks of the century, the editorship of the *Encyclopédie*, seriously tempted by the prospect of doing nothing. It was as from the depths of a profound inertia that he attempted to reassure his fiancée: "Don't worry, my Nanette, you know what I promised and I will never have any peace until I keep my word" (*C.*, I, 36).

He seems less the impassioned lover, hurtling aside the obstacles separating him from his beloved, than a beleaguered spaniel, anxiously fetching for cross-willed masters. The impression one gleans from these letters is that without Antoinette's nagging, he would have remained in Langres forever, congealed in indecision. Finally, she became exasperated to the point of heaping sarcasms upon her lover in letters which forced him to broach the dreaded subject to his family.

"Here I am in terrible straits," he reproached her, following the uproar his announcement had provoked, "until now I had hidden with considerable cunning the true object of my visit. But your impatience, which I can only praise as a proof of your love, hastened my declaration" (*C.*, I, 40).

Let us listen to Diderot's *père*'s description of what ensued. He was writing to Antoinette's mother, asking her to put an end to her daughter's unfortunate relationship with his son.

He passed with such suddenness from pleas to threats, and from threats to action, that I believed I needed to take precautions against a frenzy so harmful to your daughter and to him. If Mademoiselle your daughter is as well bred and if she loves him as much as he believes, she will exhort him to renounce her hand, for it is only at that price that he will regain his freedom, because with the aid of some friends who were shocked by his boldness, I have had him put away. We will have more than enough power, in my opinion, to keep him there until he changes his mind.

A son for whom I did everything threatens to send the sheriff after me, and you permitted it. (*C.*, I, 41–42)

His father had had him incarcerated in a monastery near Troyes, from which he escaped by a window three days later, making his way through the wintry fields back to Paris and his Antoinette. They were wed November 6, 1743, a month after his thirtieth birthday, in a clandestine ceremony. The couple moved to an obscure quarter of Paris, keeping their marriage a secret until some six years later, when Diderot's family learned of it indirectly.

A fortuitous and perhaps fortunate event had taken place during his stay in Langres which provided Diderot with a tiny bit of leverage in dealing with his monolithic family. Among other miscellaneous tasks he performed in Paris to earn a living, he had translated Temple Stanyan's *History of Greece*. The proofs arrived in the midst of the family conclaves. To Diderot's astonishment, he told Antoinette, "they are doing wonders. My father and mother, who did not seem much disposed to letting me come back [to Paris] are the first to encourage my return, convinced that I am occupied there with something useful, and disabused of I don't know how many bad stories about me they have been told" (*C.*, I, 37). An interesting development. Diderot, as the sempiternal amateur, appeared to infuriate his family, but Diderot as a man of letters merited a little respect. It was not the contents of the proofs which impressed them, but merely their existence; they were the products of some industry, no matter how alien.

Six years later, in August 1749, while he was imprisoned in Vincennes for his defense of materialism, the *Lettre sur les aveugles*, Diderot wrote a letter to M. Berryer, the Lieutenant-General of Police which, although it is a *pièce justificative*, nevertheless expresses the passivity he still felt regarding his career: "I have been in Paris for eighteen years. I spent ten of them studying mathematics and literature, living entirely unnoticed and having no desire to be known. I found myself in circumstances which led me into a marriage . . . burdened with family, I was obliged to work and profit from my labors. I devoted myself then entirely to letters" (C., I, 85 86). Considering himself "led," "burdened," and "obliged," Diderot had begun his long literary career under a variety of imperatives— not one of which, however, seemed to have been his own need to make himself heard.

On one hand, marrying a respectable woman of the petty bourgeoisie, older than himself, must have been meant as a gesture of solidarity with his father, who had chosen the same sort of wife himself. In his play *Le Père de famille*, written some fifteen years after his wedding, which his daughter Angélique claimed was based on her parents' marriage, the son asks the father how he can disapprove of the impoverished Sophie: "My mother was virtuous and beautiful, like Sophie, she was poor, like Sophie, you loved her, as I love Sophie, would you have tolerated her being wrenched from you, my Father, and have I not also a heart?" (A.-T., VII, 225). On the other hand, Diderot was well aware that since he was marrying largely out of sexual desire, ignoring all practical considerations, he was defying the patriarchal will. By taking on the responsibilities of an undowered wife, Diderot attempted, by fiat, to establish his identity as a grown man, worthy of his father's respect. But by choosing his wife on the basis of her charms and hiding the fact that they were married, he was acknowledging the puritanical disapproval of sensual pleasure which pervaded his family milieu.

Diderot's decision to marry Antoinette was as incomprehensible to his bohemian circle in Paris as to his middle-class family in Langres. His closest friend, Rousseau, considered Diderot's assumption of domestic responsibility the height of folly. Rousseau was off in Venice acting as secretary to the French Ambassador at the time of Diderot's marriage, but the two men appear to have known one another for some time before his departure. They inhabited the same world of impecunious intellectuals, existing catch-as-catch-can on the margins of Parisian society. Rousseau, one year older than Diderot, was leading a life of expedient improvisation, assuming whatever role happened to suit his whims or the circumstances in which he found himself.[17]

If Diderot often felt overwhelmed by the parental interest in his affairs, his friend Rousseau suffered from the opposite affliction. His father, a skilled artisan like Diderot's, had left his wife in Geneva after the birth of their first son, spending the next eight years in Constantinople as watchmaker in a harem. He returned to his family in 1711. The result of the reunion between Isaac Rousseau and his wife, Suzanne Bernard, was Jean-Jacques, born on June 28, 1712, an event followed almost immediately by his mother's death. During the first ten years of his life Rousseau was raised by his father, who was despondent over the loss of his wife. "He believed he saw her again in me, without being able to forget that I had taken her from him," Rousseau wrote in his *Confessions,* "he never kissed me that I didn't feel through his sighs, his convulsive clutching, that a bitter regret was mixed with his caresses, which were all the more tender for it. When he said to me: 'Jean-Jacques, let's talk about your mother,' I used to say to him: 'Very well, Father, in that case we are going to cry,' and the word alone drew tears from him. 'Ah!' he said, 'give her back to me, console me for her, fill the void she has left in my soul. Would I love you so if you were merely my son?'" (*O.c.,* I, 7).

Then one day in 1722, when Jean-Jacques was ten years

old, Isaac Rousseau quarreled with a retired captain in the streets; feeling that his honor was in question, he quit Geneva, leaving his son behind. Jean-Jacques, orphaned of his mother at birth, was now abandoned by the father who had so ambivalently clutched and kissed him through his boyhood. By the end of his life Rousseau had come to accuse almost everyone he had ever known of betraying him, believing that he was the object of a vast conspiracy, but he never blamed his father for deserting him. On the contrary, he was always careful to label the whole affair an "accident" (*O.c.*, 1, 12). By the same token, in spite of the fact that his father had left his mother alone for eight years after only ten months of wedded life, Rousseau insisted that his parents shared a lifelong passion. "They swore it," he stated in the *Confessions*, "and Heaven blessed their vow" (*O.c.*, I, 6).

Rousseau was put in the care of an uncle, whom he compared to his father as having the weaker sense of responsibility of the two. "My uncle, a pleasure-seeker like my father, was unable to be bound by his duties as [my father] was, and took little care of us" (*O.c.*, I, 25). Rousseau occasionally visited his father, who had settled nearby and remarried, but he was not invited back under the paternal roof. Instead, he was apprenticed to a watchmaker and then to an engraver. During this interval, he recounts in the *Confessions*, he experienced an abrupt loss in self-esteem, feeling that he had somehow become defective. "I was reduced mentally as well as financially to my true state as an apprentice" (*O.c.*, I, 30). "My father, when I went to see him, no longer found me his idol." For Rousseau the passage from childhood into manhood was accompanied by events which made him feel inexplicably detestable. Instead of judging his father an irresponsible parent he called himself an unlovable son.

In 1728, at the age of sixteen, he left his native city on impulse, heading into France and a lifetime of wandering. He found a protector as well as a mistress in Mme de Warens, whom he called "my good Mama," and under her tutelage renounced his religion, becoming for a time a Catholic. He odysseyed about France, Switzerland, and Italy, taking on this identity or that, dreaming of the fame he would one day enjoy as a composer and the inventor of a simplified system of musical notation. At times he opted to become an important person instantaneously, by pretending to be someone else. He passed himself off as Dudding, an English lord, or Vaussor de Villeneuve, a Parisian music teacher. He must have been a winning young man, for despite his burgeoning eccentricity he was always able to enlist the sympathies of those whom he encountered on his way.

By 1745 he had drifted to Paris. He and Diderot were soon joined in the most intense friendship, sharing one another's prospects and fortunes to the point where, when Diderot was imprisoned in Vincennes, Rousseau said that if his friend were not soon released, he would "die of despair at the foot of the wretched dungeon." [18] But as serious and even melodramatic as the tone of their relations sometimes became, the gravity was countered by a mood of giddy complicity which frequently arose between them. They shared with their bohemian circle a taste for elaborate practical jokes, some of which bordered on the incredible. Jean Catrysse describes a typical hoax, one celebrated for its ingenuity: "Palissot dangles before the eyes of the naïve Poinsinet, then a little over twenty-five years old, a job as preceptor to the royal prince of Prussia; but the prince is protestant and cannot have a Catholic preceptor; therefore Poinsinet must abjure Catholicism; our *ingénu* having complied, he is told that the police are looking for him as a renegade; he hides, not without first disguising himself as a woman. The modern reader wonders if he is not being mystified himself when he is told that poor Poinsinet went to the extreme of buying a pomade to make himself invisible."[19] Diderot and Rousseau, in their irreverent moods, imagined collaborating on a periodical to be called *Le Persifleur* (*The Tease*), and indeed the dominant impression to be gleaned from Rousseau's memories of those years is one of impenitent frivolity.[20]

Upon his return from Venice Rousseau had taken a position as tutor to the son of Mme Dupin. He spent the fall of 1747 at Chenonceaux, the Dupins' exquisite château in the Touraine, attempting to seduce the châtelaine and "growing round as a monk." He had left a mistress in Paris, however, a simple servant girl named Thérèse Levasseur. "While I was fattening up at Chenonceaux, my poor Thérèse was getting fat in a different way" (*O.c.*, I, 342).

When he went back to Paris, Rousseau found he was about to be a father. Taking the advice of the "good and sure company" at his boardinghouse next to a bordello, he decided to place the child in the Enfants trouvés, a foundling home. The other four children which Thérèse bore him were disposed of in the same way.[21]

Rousseau could not understand why his friend Diderot had chosen to burden himself with a wife: "He had a Nanette as I had a Thérèse; it was one more similarity between us. But the difference was that my Thérèse, as pretty as his Nanette, had a sweet temper and an amiable character, made to captivate an honest man, while hers, shrewish and vociferous, showed nothing to compensate for her bad education. He married her anyway, that was the right thing to do if he had promised. As for men, who had promised nothing of the kind, I was in no hurry to imitate him."[22]

But to Diderot, taking on the support of a wife and, soon after, a family, as graceless and convulsive as it appeared, was the first important step toward adult independence. Unfortunately, it became almost immediately evident that the great synthesis of roles which his marriage was supposed to produce was not possible with Antoinette Champion. Her deficiencies appear to have been the all-too-predictable mirror images of her admirable qualities. That thorny, corseted virtue which made her, in Diderot's eyes, a suitable daughter-in-law for the master cutler of Langres, rendered her quite inadequate for satisfying Diderot's sensual temperament. "I have seen an honest woman shudder with horror at the approach of her husband," he said, in a passage which according to Henry Lefebvre described his wife. "I have seen her plunge into her bath and never believe she is adequately cleansed of the stain of duty." [23]

Within weeks of his marriage he was involved with another woman. His new mistress, Mme de Puisieux, was apparently as libertine and giddy as his wife was strait-laced and dull. He earned money for his wife, whom he had persuaded to stop working, and his mistress, whose tastes were expensive,[24] by translating Robert James's *A Medicinal Dictionary*.

Diderot was deceiving his family by concealing both the extent of his freethinking and his marriage; he was deceiving his wife by his affair with Mme de Puisieux. But the image of himself as a deceitful son and an unfaithful husband does not appear to be one he could accept. In his correspondence during those years he insisted over and over that he was "an honest man," having "as much probity as anyone in the world," and that his morals were "as pure as could be" (*C.*, I, 82, 32, 87). In his search for some means to reconcile the goodness which he experienced in himself with the contemptible figure he was cutting by orthodox standards, he came across a book, published in England some fifty years earlier and by 1745 almost forgotten. It was the Earl of Shaftesbury's *Inquiry concerning Merit and Virtue*.[25] Diderot did not so much read the book as devour it, as though it had come to fill a long-aching void in his mind. He set about translating it in the following manner: "I read and reread him, I filled myself with his thoughts, and then, so to speak, I closed his book when I took up the pen. Never has someone else's work been used with such liberty" (*A.-T.*, I, 16). What he said appears to be true: he produced more of a version of Shaftesbury than a translation; the English lord's ideas were so thoroughly assimilated that they came out as Diderot's own. What Shaftesbury offered Diderot was a largely coherent system of moral values that vindicated both the passions and freedom of thought while denying the necessity of religious belief in order to be virtuous. The word *necessity* was the crux of what Shaftesbury presented, for although he claimed that religion could be of great value in leading man to morality, he showed that, strictly speaking, it could be done without. For Shaftesbury, the traditional spurs to human virtue—the promise of heaven and the threat of hell—were, like Hobbes's concept of man as *"lupus hominem,"* based on a mistaken view of human nature. He set forth the principle that far from being an egomaniacal individualist, bent only on his salvation in the one case or his solipsistic gratifications in the other, man was a creature whose true happiness lay in obeying his social instincts. Man was not intended to live alone, to work out his destiny without regard to his fellow creatures, but, on the contrary, was made to contribute to the well-being of his "system," that is, his social unit. Shaftesbury postulated an almost biological theory of man's interaction with his milieu, a view which was to be reflected in Diderot's organization of the *Encyclopédie*. Whereas Rousseau, a few years later in his two *Discours* and his *Contrat social,* was to insist upon the primal separation of human beings, social commerce representing a degradation of mankind's pristine independence, for Shaftesbury the need to function within a larger group revealed the truest aspect of human nature.

Diderot discovered in Shaftesbury the virtue of social man which he could pit against the orthodox virtue of theological man as being at once more natural and more noble. The passions were sources of positive moral good insofar as they contributed to the happiness of others; thus even that Christian bugbear, sexuality, resulted in virtue if it were permitted to follow its "natural" bent, toward a shared pleasure. "Unnatural" affections, on the other hand, produced only unhappiness, another word for vice. As proof of this assertion Shaftesbury pointed out that "even prostitutes know very well how necessary it is that everyone whom they entertain with their beauty should believe there are satisfactions reciprocal, and that pleasures are no less given than received" (*A.-T.*, I, 310).

God, while not banished from Shaftesbury's scheme of things, was assigned the role of a sublime observer, whose presence was felt by every human being not totally corrupted. He offered man "the superintendency of a Supreme Being, a witness and spectator of human life . . . conscious of whatsoever is felt or acted in the universe" (*A.-T.*, I, 268).

In translating Shaftesbury, Diderot was performing a complicated and perilous task. He was becoming the "author" of a book which repudiated The Book, putting into words a philosophy that defied the certitudes of his father's religion. But his position regarding this work was somewhat anomalous: the original words were not his own, he was merely a translator; the ultimate responsibility for the dangerous ideas presented lay with the eminent Third Earl of Shaftesbury. It was as if the prestige of the English peer provided Diderot with an imposing façade through which (in footnotes) he occasionally stuck his head to confide his own thoughts. Thus to the comment that an individual can only be considered good or bad in reference to a *system*, by which Shaftesbury meant mainly a social organization, Diderot interjected, in a fit of bravado, a diatribe against his brother's elected state of celibacy: "Divine anchorite, suspend for a moment the profundity of your meditations and lower yourself to enlighten a poor man of the world, who is proud to be one. I have passions, and I would be sorry not to have any: It is with great passion that I love my God, my King, my country, my family, my friends, my mistress, and myself. . . . If conscience reproaches one of us two for having been useless to his country, his family, and his friends, I do not fear that I will be the one" (*A.-T.*, I, 25). Having thus told Didier off, he went on to dedicate the book to him—a gesture not at all intended as an offense but rather quite sincerely as a gesture of peace. Such obtuseness about other people was characteristic of Diderot during the early years of his life.

Shaftesbury's work was Diderot's apology at the same time as his *J'accuse.* To his family's scandalized disapproval of his way of life he countered the theories of a celebrated English lord and the tentative assumption of a new persona, that of the *philosophe.* In his dedication he spoke not as the sin-ridden black sheep of an exemplary family, but as the enlightened spokesman of a higher morality. He attempted to present himself to his brother as equally virtuous and equally religious, only more profoundly so. "No Virtue without Religion; [26] no Happiness without Virtue: these are two truths which you will find investigated in these reflections which I wrote for our *common good*. Do not let this expression wound you, I know the solidity of your mind and the goodness of your heart. Accept [this work], I beg you, as the gift of a *philosophe* and the token of a brother's friendship" (*C.*, I, 52).

To call himself a *philosophe* was to transform his negation of Catholicism into an affirmation of a loftier view of the world. To be a *philosophe* was to belong to a spiritual group of great men who had fought the prejudices of their day; it was to forsake the loneliness of the merely wayward and become a member of another community, that of the enlightened. The feeling of solidarity with philosophers who had suffered for their beliefs was immensely comforting to Diderot; it enabled him to see himself not as a renegade Catholic but as one of a prestigious line of hero-martyrs in a noble cause. He could read his struggles into those of Bayle, of Spinoza, even of Socrates. He judged Seneca—who had, in his view, failed to rise to the moral challenge of dealing with Nero—as "not as honest as he is said to have been" (A.-T., I, 118). And the sense of being part of a social unit, which Diderot had lost by his rupture with his family, was recaptured by identifying with the philosophical party. The "we" of the freethinkers replaced the "we" of the family. Their virtue would become his if he could become one of them.

Shaftesbury made one other point which was of vital importance for Diderot because it enabled him to preserve a sense of his own inner goodness in the face of disapprobation. He insisted that the test of virtue was not the value of a man's acts, but the purity of his intentions. If he wished to do good his essence was virtuous, regardless of what he actually accomplished; if his heart was full of selfishness his good actions were to no avail. "Whatever advantage one has procured for society, the motive alone determines merit. Illustrate yourself by great actions all you please, you will be vicious as long as you act only through self-interest. Were you to attend to your own fortune with all possible moderation, fine, but had you no other motive in rendering to your species what you owe it through natural inclination, you are not virtuous" (A.-T., I, 30).

Diderot's version of Shaftesbury was by and large well received, even the Jesuit *Journal de Trévoux* treating it respectfully.[27] Encouraged by his success, Diderot set about writing his first original book, supposedly during Lent of 1746. *Les Pensées philosophiques* shows the marks of Diderot's double ambition: on one hand, to establish his credentials as a real *philosophe*, and, on the other, to demonstrate his personal goodness by his capacity to be scrupulously just and impartial in treating a subject that was often the occasion for fanaticism.

Les Pensées philosophiques combined in its very title Diderot's desire to enroll himself, with Pascal and Voltaire, in the ranks of the intellectually estimable.[28]

In the *Pensées* Diderot wished to establish the superior morality, not merely the superior truth, of a natural religion, founded on reason, over the perversities of revealed religion, specifically, of course, Catholicism. But he did not cast himself into the role of Christianity's prosecutor; he preferred to present himself as an impartial judge, an *homme moyen raisonable* who carefully evaluated arguments on all sides. To do this he widened the debate to include an atheistic, a deistic, and a skeptical position as well as an orthodox one. By this device he enlarged the combat between those who followed Christ and those who rejected Him into a more general *mêlée,* where the Christians represented only one persuasion among many. He turned his attention from one to the other, judiciously awarding points. He concluded the book by describing the partisans of the various positions battling one another: "I judged the blows; I held the balance between the combatants; its arms went up or down as a result of the weight each carried. After long oscillations, it tilted in the direction of the Christian, but only because his side was heavier than the other. I am my own witness to my equity. It is not my fault that the weight of the Christian side did not seem heavier to me than it did. I swear my sincerity to God" (*A.-T.,* I–II, 155).

In spite of these protestations of objectivity, the book clearly revealed the burden of Diderot's preoccupations. He began with a thrust to the very heart of the quarrel between his family and himself by defending the legitimacy of the passions against religious dogmas denigrating them. "The passions are tirelessly denounced, all of man's woes are imputed to them, and it is forgotten that they are also the source of all his pleasures. . . . Only the passions, and the great ones, are capable of elevating the soul to great things. If my life is dearer to me than my mistress, I am only an ordinary lover" (*A.-T.*, I–II, 127). Diderot was aggressively attacking his family's religious conviction that virtue lies in the abnegation of the flesh and the submission of reason to authority. But he was not yet willing publicly to label himself an atheist, although he defended the unbelieving position adroitly. He formulated a belligerent profession of faith, predicting quite accurately that it would not satisfy the "devout," although perhaps hoping that it might: "I was born in the Roman Catholic Apostolic Church; and with all my strength I submit to its decisions. I want to die in the religion of my forebears, and I believe in its validity as much as someone can who has never had any immediate contact with the Divinity, and who has never witnessed any miracle. This is my profession of faith; I am almost certain that they [the devout] will be discontented with it, although perhaps there is not one of them in a position to do better" (*A.-T.*, I–II, 153).

The book was condemned as "scandalous and contrary to religion and good morals." It was lacerated and burned at the stake by the *parlement* of Paris (*A.-T.*, I–II, 125).

A letter Diderot's father wrote a few years later shows the patriarch reaching toward his appalling son both to embrace him and to control him, the strength of his righteousness only equaled by that of his love. He had heard that Diderot's works had aroused the wrath of the authorities and he admonished him: "Consider that if God gave you talents, it was not in order for you to work at weakening the dogmas of our holy Religion. I know, my son, that no one is exempt from calumny, and that works may have been imputed to you in which you had no part; but to prove the opposite to the important people with whom you are acquainted, give the public some Christian production in your own way. This work will gain you the blessing of heaven and I will keep you in my good graces." He had learned of his son's clandestine marriage, so much against his wishes, but his reaction could not have been more reasonable and measured: "If this marriage is legitimate let the thing be done, I am satisfied" (*C*, I, 93). He enclosed the sum of one hundred fifty francs.

Immediately after *Les Pensées philosophiques* Diderot reverted to a kind of bellicose bohemianism, but just as his philosophic work was peppered with libertine examples, his libertine novel *Les Bijoux indiscrets* was heavily larded with philosophy. The central conceit, that all women, regardless of their modest façades, are actually motivated by the utmost lubricity, was not so far removed from the arguments extolling the ubiquity of the passions advanced in *Les Pensées philosophiques*. But *Les Bijoux indiscrets*, written on a bet with his mistress and published clandestinely in 1748, represented a more impudent assault upon orthodoxy than his preceding work, for it stated not merely the legitimacy of the passions, but their supremacy for half the human race: " 'I believe,' said the Sultan, 'that the "Bijou" makes a woman do a hundred things without her being aware of them; and I noticed more than once that she who believed she was following her head was obeying her bijou.' A great philosopher placed the soul, I mean the masculine one, in the pineal gland. If I were to attribute a soul to women, I know quite well where I would put it" (*O.r.*, 83).

Les Bijoux indiscrets, while insisting upon the primacy of the passions, also shows Diderot's incomprehension of their workings. In an attempt to fathom the mysteries of the other sex, Diderot has recourse to a curiously Cartesian mechanical psychology. The characters in the novel speak to one another, engage in various pastimes, relate even their dreams, but all this behavior is seen by the author as diversionary activity which does not permit communication. Only the Sultan, with his magic ring forcing the lady's vagina to speak, can know what her real experience has been. Like complicated wind-up toys, women are inexplicably opaque to everyone but him who knows the secret mechanism activating their inner voice. The characters, although sexually hyperactive, seem flat and lacking in vitality because the framework of the novel is an utter determinism. It is an impersonal world from which the author has detached himself, reporting what might have been a scientific experiment. Not yet able to come to terms with his own contradictory motives and needs, Diderot elected to view the human race as so many machines.

In *Les Bijoux indiscrets,* Diderot struck a theme which continued to reverberate through the rest of his works, that of appearances unmasked. The Sultan Mangogul, surfeited with the endless physical possession of women at his African court, wishes to penetrate the secrets of their pasts, "to know the adventures they have and have had" (*O.r.,* 8). By means of the magic ring given him by the genie Cucufa, he forces each "*bijou*" to reveal what its owner would never utter voluntarily. The "*bijou*" gives the lie to her pretensions, it speaks the truth which she attempts to conceal, even from herself, beneath her assumed role. Alphane likes to play the part of the naïve virgin, Sophie and Zélide enjoy their reputations for piety, Fulvia convinces Sélim that he is the only man she has ever loved. The Sultan throws them all into the cruelest quandary; they have no choice but to be stripped of their disguises and humiliated before their rivals. The Sultan enjoys their discomfiture and that of their lovers and husbands quite as much as the tales their "*bijoux*" tell. To his favorite's objections he replies: " 'What do I care about these disabused husbands, these lovers in despair, these women disgraced, these girls dishonored, provided I am having a good time? Am I then the Sultan for naught?' " (*O.r.,* 15).

Mangogul was but the first version of a study to which Diderot was to return again and again: that of the manipulative trickster. Mangogul is aggressive and unabashedly curious, his power to force out the truth is only an extension of his will to despotism. Some years later a depressed Diderot was to examine the unscrupulous nephew of Rameau and his hero, the renegade of Avignon, not as exotic potentates but as specimens of an unfortunately familiar species known as humanity. Ten years after *Le Neveu de Rameau* was written, however, Diderot's fear and disgust toward the ammoral trickster turned into a kind of fondness. In *Jacques le fataliste et son maître*, he displayed a certain admiration for the devious Mme de la Pommeraye. A string of lesser *persifleurs* preceded the final, full-dress depiction of the manipulative protagonist in the person of M. Hardouin, the hero of Diderot's last play, *Est-il bon? Est-il méchant?*, and the picture revealed itself to be a signed self-portrait. But of this side of his nature Diderot was largely unaware in 1748, and many years separated the philosopher from recognizing himself in the Sultan.

A curious aspect of *Les Bijoux indiscrets* was that in describing Mangogul's inquisitiveness regarding the private lives of his subjects, Diderot was drawing a recognizable sketch of both Louis XIV and Louis XV. Both monarchs were accustomed to receiving a nightly report from police headquarters detailing the scandalous trivia as well as the major events of the day. Besides the regular police force, the Chief of Police in Paris employed more than three thousand spies in his region alone. Their function is summarized in a document dating from 1753, a kind of official account book for the city from that year: "Appointments of three thousand spies spread through the city, the suburbs, and the environs of Paris to find out everything that happens, many at twenty sous a day, most at ten, not including remuneration for those making discoveries, which remunerations are not fixed but go according to the value of the aforementioned discoveries." [29]

The spies came from all levels of society, but the water

carrier's story of low-life debauchery was as fascinating to the King of France as the more elegant gossip of his ranking snoop, the Prince de Carignan. M. de Pontchartrain, the minister whose job it was to read the King his evening news, instructed the Police Chief to relate even the smallest details of love affairs because "they give pleasure in the telling," and "even indifferent matters may amuse the king."[30] Diderot's Mangogul, therefore, although draped in African ceremonial robes, was at heart a Bourbon. He shared with the penultimate Louis the belief that knowledge is the prerogative of power.

Diderot was apparently surprised that the novel was not favorably received. In response to the criticism of Mme de P. (Prémontval) he wrote: "I shall not counter your reproaches with the example of Rabelais, of Montaigne, of Swift, and of a few others I could name, who attacked the follies of their times in the most cynical way and retained the title of 'sage' " (C., I, 56). He felt misunderstood. He had enrolled himself in the ranks of the enlightened; why wasn't the effect of his libertine writings the same as that of his masters? Convinced of the purity of his intentions, the disapproval his behavior elicited in other people astonished and depressed him.

Unable to anticipate the quite predictable antagonism he aroused, he was deeply hurt, for example, when his brother refused to accept his claims for the superior moral status of the skeptic. In a letter to Didier he accused him of being contentious and fanatical, assuring him that "if these are the two qualities which your religion provides, I am very happy with mine [he had crossed out "not to have any" and replaced it with "mine"], and I hope not to change it. As for the need which you believe one has of it in order to be an honest man, if you feel such a need, too bad for you" (C., I, 221). Despite his peremptory tone, Diderot was by no means ready to acknowledge a stalemate in the battle with his brother over moral superiority. After *Les Bijoux indiscrets* he abandoned the licentious tale, having begun to direct his moral fervor and philosophical convictions into the more effective channel of the *Encyclopédie*.

2/Philosophy and Power

In 1747 Diderot was still a rather obscure free-lance writer whose earnings scarcely sufficed to support his wife and infant son, François, and to satisfy the whims of his mistress, Mme de Puisieux. His friend Rousseau's existence showed even less promise than his own; he had written nothing substantial and had settled into a rather disreputable ménage with the simple Thérèse. Friedrich Melchior Grimm, soon to become Diderot's closest friend and most powerful ally, was still a mere youth writing his thesis in Latin for a degree from the University of Leipzig.

It is remarkable how, in a few brief years, these three men rose to a level of international influence unprecedented among men of letters, by no other means than their pens and their wits. Rousseau would not only turn down pensions and gifts from Louis XV, George III, and Frederick of Prussia, he would be invited to draft a new constitution for Poland and to visit Corsica for the purpose of becoming its *Législateur*, or lawgiver.[1] Grimm refused Catherine of Russia's offer to be Minister of Education but accepted the title of Captain in her army, the Polar Star from the Queen of Sweden, and a plenipotentiary ministry from the Duke of Saxe-Gotha.[2] Diderot encountered great difficulty in his later years breaking the emotional bear hug in which the Empress of Russia was constantly threatening to enfold him with costly gifts. When he visited her in Saint Petersburg he became so annoyed by the reverence every provincial court paid him along the way that he arranged to lose his trunk, and sent word that he could not properly appear in his one remaining garment—a nightshirt.

The crowned heads vied with one another to patronize Diderot, Grimm, and Rousseau as well as their lesser associates. It was a strange spectacle; the greatest, richest, and most powerful sovereigns in the world struggling to possess the free-thinking *philosophes* as ardently as if they were rare jewels or neighboring countries.

Almost without exception, ruling princes in the second half of the eighteenth century shared a need to be seen as modern, enlightened, and civilized.[3] No sovereign, whether it was Frederick of Prussia or Leopold of Tuscany, wanted to appear a splendid Gothic terror as his grandfather had. In some instances the desire for a progressive image was even accompanied by authentic efforts at reform. In Austria under Maria Theresa and Joseph II, real, if limited progress was made in modernizing the bureaucracy and establishing laws of toleration. Maria Theresa's son, the Grand Duke Leopold, abolished capital punishment in Tuscany for a time and also rationalized the tax structure. Similar attempts to reorganize legal systems according to the principles of reason and justice were made by Charles III in Spain and Gustaf in Sweden. In the case of other sovereigns, however, one has the impression that the appearance of modernity was a thin veneer over the most frighteningly archaic of kingships. Prince Paul of Russia, for example, is said to have given a poor poet two thousand serfs as thanks for dedicating a poem to him. A Bronze Age royalty, forcing its shaggy head into a powdered wig, brought up the rear of a parade of sovereigns who wished to be known as "modern." Almost without exception, the ruling princes of sound mind coveted the appearance, if not the substance, of virtue.

The rulers' ambitions set the tone for their courts. By and large, in the closing decades of the eighteenth century, some degree of literary sophistication, philosophical skepticism, and political liberalism was a *sine qua non* of elegance in Europe's capitals. The great illiterate brute with the blood of battle on his sword and mud from the boar hunt caked to his boots had ceased to be anybody's hero. Sébastien Mercier, who professed no particular admiration for Diderot or Grimm, nevertheless summed up the power of the *philosophes* in the following terms: "If despotism has become civilized, if the sovereigns have begun to fear the voice of the nations, to respect that supreme tribunal, it is to the writer's pen that we owe this new and hitherto unknown restraint. What ministerial or royal iniquity can be imagined going unchecked these days? And does not the glory of kings depend upon the sanction of the *philosophe*?" [4]

It was in this climate that Diderot, Grimm, and to some extent Rousseau were able to make themselves heard; and for a considerable period of time the voice of the philosophers in Paris caught the conscience of the King.

The direction of two complementary enterprises, Diderot's *Encyclopédie* and Grimm's *Correspondance littéraire, philosophique et critique,* gave the philosophers an opportunity to disseminate and elaborate their new ideas. Diderot's connection with the *Encyclopédie* began as one more free-lance assignment, having, in his mind, no more pith or moment than his translation of James's *A Medicinal Dictionary.* The publisher Le Breton had made arrangements with an eccentric literary entrepreneur named Gua de Malves to translate an English dictionary, Ephraim Chambers' *Cyclopaedia,* but the project limped along for a bit, then came to a dead halt. On October 16, 1747, Le Breton approached Diderot and the mathematician d'Alembert and asked them to assume direction of the work. By the time all thirty-five volumes had been published in 1780, Chambers' *Cyclopaedia* had long since been swallowed and forgotten, and Diderot's wish, that the *Encyclopédie* might "change the ordinary way of thinking," was in large measure realized.

The editorship of the *Encyclopédie*, despite Diderot's incessant complaints about the staggering burden of work it imposed, was the ideal catalyst for his energies and his genius. Before assuming the task of organizing the enterprise, Diderot seemed centerless, his works mainly translations or pastiches. In becoming the center of the *Encyclopédie* Diderot was forced to define himself, and his definition gave him a coherence which was to prove useful, until it became so constraining that it was jettisoned. The editor of the *Encyclopédie* was, in Diderot's words, "a man endowed with great sense, celebrated for the breadth of his knowledge, the loftiness of his sentiments and his ideas, and his love for work; a man loved and respected for his character, both domestic and public" (*A.-T.*, XIV, 502). Although this was not the wayward son his family in Langres would have immediately recognized, for Diderot it provided a kind of model against which he could measure himself.

The obscure recipient of a publisher's bounty became a patron himself, assigning articles to appropriate contributors, and this change from the passive and responsibility-free role to the active one seemed to bring his personality into sharper focus. Having to weigh each contributor's words in terms of their value to his enterprise put him in a position rather like that of his father, who parceled out various steps in the fabrication of his instruments, and thus "controlled a large number of boutiques and workshops in the whole area of

Langres."[5] Diderot began referring to the *Encyclopédie* as the "philosophical boutique" and seemed to find this conception of himself as an intellectual master craftsman congenial.[6] He frequently selected contributors because of their practical experience with the matter to be discussed. Dr. Théodore Tronchin, for example, the Swiss inventor of a smallpox vaccine, wrote the article on "Inoculation," Quesnay, the Physiocrat, prepared the article on "Grains," and Diderot engaged a silk worker, Bonnet, to describe the process of making velvet. Rousseau assumed responsibility for the parts dealing with music and d'Alembert for those concerning mathematics. The assignment of other topics, such as "Fornication" to Voltaire, was perhaps based less on expertise than on the contributor's reputation for wit and style.

All in all some 142 names were listed in the prefaces to the various volumes as having collaborated in the enterprise. The work as a whole, however, and above all the first six volumes, reflected the personality and the intentions of Diderot himself. He was responsible for the long, major pieces which gave the work its indelible stamp, among them "Bible," "Cynics," "Eclecticism," and "Encyclopedia."

Diderot never conceived the *Encyclopédie* as an inert compendium of scholarship, meekly offering impartial definitions to the public. It is this aspect which unsettles the modern reader who assumes objectivity to be of the essence in reference works. For Diderot the *Encyclopédie* was from its very inception infused with great moral significance. It was not to lie still and permit itself to be used, but it was supposed to collar the reader, to lead or even drag him through its pages for his own moral improvement. In the article "Encyclopedia," which appeared in Volume IV (1754), Diderot described his vision of the editor's function: "We must . . . inspire a taste for science, a horror of falsehood and vice, and a love of virtue, because everything which does not ultimately aim at happiness and virtue is nothing" (*A.-T.*, XIV, 461).

The virtue toward which Diderot as editor would escort humanity was not, however, either a Platonic ideal or a Christian obedience to God's will. The *Encyclopédie* was to make people better in the only capacity which mattered: as citizens. From beginning to end, it is an astonishing monument to the belief in group responsibility. In every article, from "Tyrant" to "Maceration," the referent is civil utility. *The philosophes* served mankind by trying to convince it that society was its proper idol. If persuasion, or the appeal to reason, should fail, then seduction, or the manipulation of the passions, was deemed legitimate, because, as the article "Philosopher" pointed out, for the philosopher "civil society is, so to speak, a divinity on earth; he honors it by his probity, by a scrupulous attention to his duties, and by the sincere desire not to be a useless or burdensome member of it. He is 'kneaded,' as it were, with the leavening of order and rule; he is filled with ideas of the good of civil society, of which he knows the principles better than other men" (*A.-T.*, XIV, 276–77).

Diderot, thus seeing himself in a Messianic role, devoted much thought to making the *Encyclopédie* an effective instrument for the amelioration of mankind. What his mind gradually developed was a cunning contraption that would lay hold of the readers, not letting them go until they had been re-educated and ennobled. The unwary who entered the work for a clear-cut discussion of "Taxes," or "Agnus Dei," would be enticed by the references at the end of the article to plunge ahead and lose themselves in the philosophic way of thinking. The encyclopedic education could thus begin with any of the thousands of entries which one's curiosity prompted one to consult.

Diderot's *machine infernale*, for all the defects to which such an unwieldy undertaking is subject, realized its creator's ambitions. It was then, as it remains to this day, a uniquely fascinating work, often so well written and artfully arranged that its perusal can addict the reader. Whether he travels as Diderot intended, entering the work at any point and following the thread of references, from "Liberty," for example, to "Monarchy," from "Monarchy" to "Morals," from "Morals" to "Representative," and from "Representative" to "Tyrant," or whether he simply pursues his own train of thought, the journey is full of unpredictable turns.

Diderot exercised great ingenuity to make the work enticing. The *Encyclopédie*'s most powerful ally in educating the public was its curiosity, and Diderot appealed to the lower elements in that curiosity as well as to the more elevated. He varied the tone and the content of the articles in unexpected ways, sometimes introducing coarse or titillating material in unlikely places, and, conversely, often using a promisingly racy rubric as the pretext for denouncing an enemy or elaborating a serious argument. The entries frequently omit the perfunctory details most dictionary editors feel obliged to provide, and go directly to the piquant. A brief article on "Ceylon," for example, is devoted almost exclusively to the exotic sexual mores of that country's inhabitants. We learn, among other local customs, that the Ceylonese bride gives "the first night to the husband, the second to his brother, and if there is a third or fourth brother, all the way to seven, each has his own night; thus one woman suffices for an entire family" (*A.-T.,* XIV, 40).

But the reader who anticipated a bit of fun in the article "Prostitute" might have been surprised to discover the following denunciation of Fréron, a critic of the *Encyclopédie:* "The meaning of the words *prostitute* and *prostitution* has been extended to include critics such as we have today, at the head of whom one can place the odious personage [Fréron]; and it has been said of these writers that they *prostitute* their pens for money, for favor, for lies, for envy and for the vices most unworthy of a well-bred man" (*A.-T.,* XVI, 440). Anything could be the pretext for attacking the unenlightened or defending the philosophers. The interjection "Oh" was the occasion for the following bit of pointed business: "Oh, interject. augm. (Gram.) *Oh.* don't doubt it! *Oh, oh,* I have other principles than those you imagine I have, and I am not one person in my writings and another in my conduct.

> He spoke so well of wars,
> Of the earth, the sphere and the stars,
> Of civil laws and canon laws,
> He understood things by effect and by cause
> Was he an honest man? *Oh,* no." [7]

The excitement and willful perversity of the *Encyclopédie* were only occasionally ends in themselves; chiefly they served to captivate the reader so that he would submit to the moral retraining which Diderot felt was the work's real function. The articles bearing on politics, philosophy, economics, history, and theology all shared a common goal: they were to destroy the old, habitual mental associations of the public and forge new ones instead. Rather than link the word "King" to "God" and "Father" as he was accustomed to do by tradition, the reader of the *Encyclopédie* would be led to associate "King" with ideas like "Tyrant" and "Despot." Outmoded concepts had to be destroyed by the process of redefining a great part of the average person's abstract vocabulary. While no single article could change the public's mode of thinking, thousands of entries, absorbed over a period of years, would cumulatively undermine the old intellectual order. Political subjects were treated in long articles like "Citizen" and "Representative" but even the briefest piece could add its buckshot to the charge. The following definition of the word "Indigent" shows how such entries were used to drive home the message of society's injustice:

Indigent: a man who lacks the necessities of life in the midst of his fellow men who are enjoying, with offensive luxury, all the possible superfluities. One of the most unfortunate results of bad administration is to divide society into two classes of men, one opulent, the other wretched. *Indigence* is not a vice; it's worse. A vicious person is invited out, we shrink from the *indigent*. He is seen only with his open hand extended. There are no *indigents* among the savages.

At the end of the article the reader is referred to "People," and if he is docile he will discover that the only class which still permits itself to be called "the people" consists of the workers. As for the financiers, "those rich and curious men, nothing escapes them, not flowers from Italy, nor parrots from Brazil, nor grotesques from China, nor porcelains from Saxe, from Sèvres, or from Japan. You see their palaces in town and country, their tasteful clothing, their elegant furniture—does all that smell like the *people*? That man who was able to force fortune through finance eats in one meal the food for a hundred families of the *people*." Nevertheless, the article concludes, "the *people* form the most numerous and important part of the nation." [8]

By sending the reader from "Indigent" to "People," Diderot established a connection to which the public was not accustomed. These "references," in Diderot's words, tended

to juxtapose ideas, to contrast principles; to attack, shake up, and secretly reverse the ridiculous opinions one would dare not insult directly. A great art and a great advantage might be found in [these] references. The whole work could acquire an internal force and a secret utility, of which the effects would surely be felt in the long run. Each time, for example, that a national prejudice had to be treated with respect, it should be exposed dutifully in its own article, with its entire array of reasonableness and appeal; but the edifice of mud will be overturned, the vain cloud of dust dissipated by referring to those articles where opposing truths are based upon solid principles. This means of enlightening men works very promptly upon good minds; and it operates infallibly and without harmful side effects, secretly and silently on all minds. If these "references" . . . are anticipated in advance and skillfully prepared [by the editor], they will give the *Encyclopédie* the characteristic a good dictionary must have: of changing the ordinary way of thinking. (*A.-T.*, XIV, 462–63)

It is interesting to observe how often Diderot used the words "secret" and "secretly" in these passages. The "references" will "secretly reverse . . . opinions," endowing the *Encyclopédie* with a "secret utility," and the process works "secretly and silently on all minds." Yet he published these remarks quite openly in the article "Encyclopedia." [9]

The missionary role he assumed led Diderot, little by little, into an awkward position. In condemning the *Encyclopédie* as an instrument designed to subvert the values of society, its enemies merely upheld a view expressed by its editor. They marshaled themselves for the battle, aiming their sharpest blows at Diderot. Since he had used so many pages of the *Encyclopédie* to record his enthusiasm for virtue, his critics countered by denouncing him as a fraud, "an unscrupulous metaphysician," "a compiler without probity." In his *Année littéraire*, Elie Fréron, a plausible and talented member of the opposition, repeatedly accused Diderot of plagiarizing. The Jesuits impugned Diderot's morals in their *Journal de Trévoux*, and the Jansenists did them one better: they created a whole publication, *Le Censeur hebdomadaire*, just to point out the errors of the *Encyclopédie* and the depravity of its editor.

If Diderot frequently felt surrounded by enemies, he could console himself with the knowledge that he enjoyed the protection of a powerful ally in Melchior Grimm. Grimm had become the editor of a literary newsletter whose influence on the intellectual life of Europe was incalculable, and this despite a circulation never exceeding thirty. Its subscribers tell the tale of its success, for the Princess Palatine, the Prince of Hesse-Darmstadt, the Grand Duke of Tuscany, the Empress Catherine II of Russia, and King George III of England all received Grimm's frequent accounts of events in the French literary world through the handwritten, clandestine publication. The *Correspondance littéraire,* in short, was designed for the exclusive delectation of the crowned heads of Europe. In Grimm's words: "For a long time I have made it a rule to give this *Correspondance* only to princes." [10] But a few commoners managed to get on the list of subscribers. Horace Walpole, for example, and one "Mozart, chapel master," are noted as being charged six livres a year. Catherine of Russia, on the other hand, paid 1500 francs. All in all, the *Correspondance littéraire* brought Grimm a comfortable income, although its very existence was unsuspected in Paris except among his closest friends.

Winters could be excruciating in Weimar and Saint Petersburg, but subscribers to the *Correspondance littéraire* basked in Parisian talk-of-the-town. The royal readers would know, before anyone else at court, how Voltaire's latest tragedy had been received, or what opinion one ought to hold of Helvétius's book *De l'esprit.* It was almost as good as being at Versailles, and on those delicious but painful occasions when one did visit the court par excellence, at least it was possible to appear before Louis without feeling too much the provincial bumpkin.

Grimm used the *Correspondance littéraire* to bolster the *philosophes* and to denigrate their enemies. Each volume of the *Encyclopédie* was given an elaborate review to whet the readers' appetites, while works of the opposition were dismissed with a condescending yawn.[11] In Grimm's most perfunctory remarks about Diderot he seldom called him anything less complimentary than "the Socrates of the century." He compared a dialogue written by Diderot to a conversation with Plato or Cicero. "The philosopher Diderot of the eighteenth century has no less illumination in his intellect, warmth in his imagination, nor virtue in his heart than these great men of antiquity" (*C.l.*, II, 166). At times his descriptions verged on apotheosis. In January 1757 the princes of Europe might have taken some chill out of their bones by reading the following sketch of the *Encyclopédie*'s editor: "I found my philosopher, he was alone and in one of those moments of calm, of serenity, and of enlightenment which ordinarily follow the search for truth, the contemplation of nature and the mediation of her beauties. By his facial features, animated by the most seductive imagination, I recognized the apostle of truth, which in each century inspires a tiny number of superior men" (*C.l.*, II, 140).

If Grimm waxed adulatory when he spoke of Diderot, his tone became rather crisp when he addressed himself to his subscribers. Far from avoiding ideas which might offend his titled readers, Grimm never hesitated to rap their jeweled knuckles, exhorting them to be more enlightened despots or suffer the *philosophes*' contempt. Reigns would be judged according to the virtue of the rulers, he warned his readers in August 1756: "A great lesson for the princes, which they do not seem to have sufficiently grasped! They must compensate for the favor of their birth by great virtues and superior qualities" (*C.l.*, II, 68).

From time to time Grimm evaluated various sovereigns, and he was not indulgent. If his friend Diderot was Socrates, "Louis XIV was a man without wits, rather inclined toward the great things, but a pedant" (*C.l.*, II, 69). He scolded the royals for indulging in blood sports, calling the hunt "the shameful and culpable occupation of a madman, a hundred times more savage than the beast he pursues, who, scorning the laws of nature, endlessly troubles its order and harmony."

Grimm nevertheless concluded, with a laborious chuckle, "I am not at all in agreement with the opinion of citizen Rousseau, who, in his excess of bile, says that princes should be allowed to hunt lest they do something worse" (*C.l.*, II, 114–115).

Amazingly enough, the sovereigns with few exceptions (Frederick of Prussia among them) loved being admonished. It must have made pious monarchists, like Diderot's brother, blanch to observe the French aristocracy and most of European royalty assiduously courting men who affected such scorn for the prestige of cross and crown. As Palissot observed, the "great" resemble "the women of Moscow, who only make love when they are being beaten. Some of the 'great' accorded their consideration precisely because [the *philosophes*] refused to show them any." [12]

The *philosophes'* enemies were quick to point out how Diderot, Grimm, and their friends appointed themselves and one another to the role of humanity's tutors. Palissot drew the public's attention to their system of flattering each other in print, implying that the reputation for virtue and wisdom which they enjoyed in some circles was only the result of a clever public relations campaign. "What most annoyed the small number of sensible people who in silence weigh and evaluate reputations was the literary throne these gentlemen erected for themselves, and the tacit convention between them and society which said: 'No one has a mind except us and our friends.'" [13]

More vicious was J.-B. Moreau's witty and well-aimed lampoon of the *encyclopédistes,* whom he called "Cacouacs," which the *Mercure de France* published in 1757. In addition to presenting the *encyclopédistes'* ideas in the most sinister light, Moreau denounced their morals: "The most barbarous men ever discovered have some moral qualities, the most disagreeable insects, the most venomous reptiles have some useful properties. This is not the case with the Cacouacs: their whole substance is venom and corruption; they are perhaps the only beings in nature which do evil precisely for the sake of doing evil." [14]

Between Grimm's praise and his adversaries' slander, Diderot began to lose his bearings. It was as if a private question, whether he could be called "good" if he were not religious, had grown into a frighteningly public debate. From all over Europe, voices were raised in defense or in condemnation of Diderot's virtue; he had managed to place the question of his own moral worth squarely in the center of the battle of the Enlightenment.

Diderot reacted to these pressures by taking a step backward. He began to renew his ties with Langres, attempting to make himself once more acceptable to his family and old friends, as if philosophy were merely an indifferent métier he had chosen while living in Paris, one which he had practiced rather successfully. He wrote to Mme Caroillon La Salette, an old family friend whose son would some years later wed Diderot's daughter, using a local dialect to assure her: "No matter what I did, I would never be anybody but 'Deniseu Didereut,' son of master Didier 'Didereut,' cutler at the sign of the pearl at Langres" (C., I, 143). He became involved in efforts to aid his family's friends, using the influence he had acquired in Paris, and in 1755 he was apparently ready to leave Paris and return to his home town to share his glory and his earnings with his family. But the center of his interest remained his father. "I shall continue my work with a very agreeable perspective," he wrote to him, "the pleasure of going to live by your side, and of bringing you, besides a legitimately acquired reputation, a somewhat more solid and substantial token of the good use to which I have put my time, of the life

I owe to you, of the education you have given me. Isn't it true, dear Father, that this will be a very sweet future?" (*C.*, I, 180).

In this same letter, where Diderot offered himself up for reintegration in the family, he stated the necessary condition of his return. He wanted his father to accept him as the enlightened authority on matters of faith and morals. He argued that his father spent too much time in church, which was bad for his health, and that he would serve God better by helping the poor. "I would prefer that in the evening you count the number of those you have aided than the number of masses you have heard or the psalms you have read. One must fulfill the duties of religion without question. But as for the supererogatory works which we impose on ourselves, and which are left to our discretion, since we derive no merit of obedience from them, let us attempt to compensate for this disadvantage by the excellence of our choice. Woe be to your children if they ever regret the money you use to satisfy the goodness of your heart in this world and to assure your place in the next" (*C.*, I, 181).

In showing his father that he was at the same time most concerned about his health and not in the least about his money, Diderot sought to rout his brother, Didier, a theology student of rather mercenary inclinations then in Paris. One senses that if his father could have only once accepted his son's philosophic interpretation of Christian obligation, the Palissots, Frérons, and Moreaus of the world would have mattered little to Diderot. But in the face of his father's intransigent orthodoxy, he grew increasingly uncertain of himself. He wrote to Caroillon La Salette in January 1755, pressing him to talk about his father's attitude or at least to speculate. "You don't say anything about the dear father. Is he drinking, walking, sleeping, does he play cards, does he go to church, does he pray to God, does he still want to be boss? In a word, what do you make of him? Answer this part, please" (*C.*, I, 190).

It was during this period—with a storm raging over the *Encyclopédie*, with friends praising him as a martyr to philosophy, with enemies execrating him as a public corrupter, and with his father withholding approval of his moral autonomy—that Diderot decided to become a dramatist. Abandoning for the moment all hope of gaining moral leadership in his family and the world by his intellectual endeavors, he set about writing plays which would demonstrate, if not the brilliance of his mind, at least the goodness of his heart. "What can I do," he asked his father while he was writing *Le Fils naturel* and *Le Père de famille*, "except to take such precautions that in the future slander, malice, even scrupulousness will find nothing to criticize in what I do. That is what I promise you. I beg you to believe that it is impossible for me to be happy with myself as long as you are not" (*C.*, II, 20).

The two plays show the effect of this chastened mood. Intended less to amuse the public than to wring from it an acknowledgment of the author's inner goodness, they are afflicted with self-conscious stiffness. Diderot sugared his naturally raw imagination and sardonic wit in creating these two plays; the result was treacle. *Le Fils naturel* consists of a preface, a play, and three "*entretiens*," or discussions between Dorval and "Moi." Since Dorval, the hero of the play, is also supposed to be its author, dramatizing events in his own life, the "*entretiens*" are in effect discussions between two versions of Diderot himself. But multiplying his persona did not enrich his play. It is less flesh which Dorval lends to Diderot's self-idealization than the pallid simulacrum of the wax museum.

Dorval, Constance, and Rosalie, the earnest triangle of *Le Fils naturel*, are not interesting characters because the outcome of their struggle between virtue and the passions is totally determined in advance. Since their sole *raison d'être* is

Diderot's need to make his own presence felt in the play as a man of unimpeachable probity, they seem without individuality. Diderot was willing to express only the highest imaginable human motivations, and thus deprived of ballast, the characters give the impression of floating over the stage.

Diderot could not understand why his brother refused to accept the play as proof of his good intentions. A letter of November 29, 1757, demonstrates the mixture of subservience and arrogance which continued to dominate the tone of his relations with his family:

I hear, dear brother, that my last work annoyed you a great deal. If that is the case, I would like not to have written it at all. But what could there have been in it to offend you? For your satisfaction and mine, put me in a position either to defend myself or accuse myself. Tell me frankly what displeased you. You know that I am a good man and that I am not looking for an occasion to boast but rather to justify myself in your mind, if that is possible. In the meantime, dear friend, don't trust your own insights concerning this genre, and rest assured that you won't find anything much to object to that I will not immediately be able to find examples of in works which have not been criticized. (*C*, II, 21–22)

Unable to come to grips with the central conflicts of his own personality and therefore finding it difficult to comprehend others, Diderot had recourse to the construction of models from which he hoped to unravel the mysteries of human behavior. In his essay on dramatic poetry, written the year after *Le Fils naturel,* he described his attempts to conceptualize the ideal *philosophe* with whom he could identify. "Ariste" was a man "severe in his morals, austere and simple in his speech, the mantle of the ancient philosopher was almost the only thing he lacked; for he was poor and happy in his poverty." People called Ariste a philosopher; they turned to him for judgments on the nature of the good, the true, and the beautiful. But he felt inadequate to pronounce upon these issues because within himself he observed only flux, inconstancy, and "perpetual vicissitude." The solution which Diderot proposed was to form an *ideal man* from "component parts found in nature." "But," the philosopher objected, "this man will be of my own making." "What does it matter," he answered himself, "if I create him according to invariable elements" (*A.-T.*, VII, 390–392).

Diderot began his construction of the ideal man not from the inside, from the central core of his psychic organization, but from the outside. The personality was to be deduced from the skin. "I see at first glance that since the ideal man for whom I am searching is a composite as I am, classical sculptors, by determining the proportions which they considered the most beautiful, have in part made my model. . . . Yes. . . . Let us take this statue and animate it. . . . Give it the most perfect organs that a man could have. Endow it with all the qualities that it is given to a mortal to possess, and our ideal model will be made. . . ." (*A.-T.*, VII, 392–93).

Throughout this passage Diderot hesitated, wavering between the fascination of his ideal man and his awareness of the inadequacy of the metaphor. He sought to reject his inner self as amorphous and unfathomable. Like the women in *Les Bijoux indiscrets*, who remained inscrutable until one found the mechanical key to their feelings, the ideal man was not an organic human being but a kind of super-Cartesian machine. One grasped his inner life only through his outer manifestations; physical perfection was the visible sign of moral excellence.

In his anxiety to cut the figure of an ideal *philosophe*, Diderot repudiated his sensuality and aggressiveness as inappropriate to the model, with the result that he often found himself incomprehensible. This difficulty in experiencing his own psychic life directly caused him to view other people as equally opaque. By means of such devices as the push button activating the voice of female sexuality, or the ideal man modeled on Classical sculpture, Diderot was attempting to force a recognizable pattern on the mysteries of the human mind. This drastic reduction of the inner life resulted in the statuelike quality of the characters in Le Fils naturel and Le Père de famille. The critical side of his personality, aware of his characters' marmoreal demeanor, tried to produce an illusion of reality by giving the actors detailed descriptions of the gestures and attitudes he believed would express the feelings they were intended to convey. But since the characters were always seen from the outside, like a room full of Condillac's statuary animated, their postures and grimaces only heightened the spectators' malaise.

Despite Diderot's Herculean efforts, the plays did not achieve what he had hoped they would. His father, far from finding in them the suitable employment of Christian talent to which he had exhorted his son, apparently expressed his displeasure. The Abbé Didier commented on Le Fils naturel: "I have enough [insight] to see that it is not in a comedy that one should treat religion, that you introduce it into yours apropos of nothing, and that you speak of it in an unsuitable way" (C., II, 23).

Diderot's dream that his plays would make him a moral paragon in the eyes of his family and the public was shattered. Not only did his father and brother refuse to swallow his skepticism, even sugar-coated with exemplary ethics and fervent sentiment, but Le Fils naturel was severely censored, Diderot was accused of plagiarizing Goldoni, and a nasty, potentially dangerous preface insulting two influential women was added to an edition of the work without his knowledge.[15] Depressed by the attacks mounting against him on all sides, he wrote to Voltaire: "I do not know what opinion the public will have of my dramatic talent and I hardly care, but I wanted them to see a man who carried, at the bottom of his heart, the image of virtue and the sentiment of humanity profoundly engraved, and they will have seen it" (*C.*, III, 292). But the public appeared to have seen only two mediocre comedies, one of which Voltaire ungraciously dismissed as "a wretched play about a bastard."

Le Fils naturel had another serious consequence for Diderot; it occasioned the definitive rupture between him and Jean-Jacques Rousseau. Relations between the two men had been under considerable strain for a long time. Diderot, wedged into an uncomfortable marriage for the sake of some dim vision of himself as husband and father, had seen his first four children die before they reached the age of five. Angélique, born in 1753, when her mother was forty-three years old, was the couple's only child to reach maturity. According to her memoirs, her mother dedicated her to the Virgin and always dressed her in white as a token of gratitude. The first decade of marriage must have been a bleak period for the unhappy couple, what with Mme Diderot's sickly pregnancies and the repeated deaths. It could not have helped Diderot's spirits to witness, during this protracted family agony, his friend Jean-Jacques casually depositing his own five children in an orphanage. As Rousseau commented in the *Confessions,* "I made no mystery of my conduct, not only because I was never able to hide anything from my friends but because I really saw nothing wrong with it. All things considered, I chose for my children the best, or what I believed to be the best. I would have wished, and I still would wish to have been raised and nourished as they were" (*O.c.*, I, 358).

Diderot, a man often taxed with indiscretion, never published his friend's secret, even after Rousseau attacked him in a publicly humiliating way. (Nor did the scandal-mongering Grimm, who came to detest Rousseau, although he alluded to the matter vaguely in an article about Rousseau's career in the *Correspondance littéraire:* "His private and domestic life would not be less curious [than his public one], but it is inscribed in the memory of two or three former friends whose self-respect prevents them from writing it anywhere" [*C.l.*, III, 178].) But watching his friend indulge in the irresponsibility which Diderot still had to restrain within himself was not pleasant. Diderot expressed his resentment obliquely, by failing to appear at rendezvous, then excusing himself on the grounds of family obligations. Rousseau, sequestered in the country, refused to come to Paris, and Diderot felt that having to do all the traveling for their meeting was unfair. He wanted Rousseau to appreciate the life of hard work and self-sacrifice he was leading: "It is true," Diderot wrote in March 1757, "that for fifteen years I have had a wife, child, domestic, no money, and that my life is so full of difficulty and pain that sometimes I cannot enjoy the few hours of happiness and relaxation I promised myself. According to their characters, my friends make of this a subject for pleasantries or insults" (*C.*, I, 234).

Rousseau, however, received these cries for pity and admiration like a stone wall. "When you make arrangements, you are not unaware that you have wife, child, domestic, etc. But you make them as if nothing might force you to break them; thus I am right to admire your courage" (*C.*, I, 236). Although Rousseau had disapproved of Diderot's marriage from the beginning, and it may be inferred that Diderot held no very high opinion of his friend's relations with Thérèse Levasseur, their belief in their temperamental twinship survived every proof to the contrary until, at last, it came athwart Rousseau's "intellectual and moral reform."

Rousseau's first works, the *Discours sur les sciences et les arts* (1750) and the *Discours sur l'origine et les fondements de l'inégalité parmi les hommes* (1754), although loosely categorized as "philosophic," were profoundly alien to the whole

Encyclopedic spirit, insisting as they did that civilization, with its social ties, its deferral of gratification, and its emphasis upon the abstract, was the enemy rather than the savior of mankind.

The two works, produced in a trancelike state of enthusiasm, abruptly lifted Rousseau from a warm if squalid anonymity and hurtled him into world fame. "The success of my first works had made me fashionable," he related in his *Confessions*. "My way of life excited curiosity. People wanted to make the acquaintance of this bizarre man who sought out no one and cared only to live freely and happily in his own way: that was enough to make it impossible for him to do so. My room never emptied itself of those who, under various pretexts, came to grab hold of my time. The women used a thousand ruses to have me for dinner. The ruder I was to people, the more stubborn they became" (*O.c.*, I, 367). At first he found his epiphany exhilarating. The austere "sage" he had represented himself to be in the two discourses now stared back at him from the eyes of an adoring public. His adolescent dream of becoming a great man from one moment to the next had been realized, and Rousseau embraced the illusion he himself had created.

I was really transformed; my friends, my acquaintances no longer recognized me. I was no longer the man, timid and ashamed rather than modest, who dared neither present himself nor speak, who was disconcerted by a playful word, who blushed at a woman's glance. Audacious, proud, intrepid, everywhere I carried an assurance all the firmer in that it was simple and resided more in my heart than in my demeanor. The scorn which my profound meditations had inspired in me for the morals, the maxims, and the prejudices of my century rendered me insensible to the mockery of those who shared them, and I crushed their little witticisms with my phrases as I would crush an insect between my fingers. What a change! All Paris was repeating the sharp and biting sarcasms of the same man who two years earlier and ten years later was never able to find what he wanted to say nor the word he needed to use. (*O.c.*, I, 416–17)

As long as he stayed in Paris he remained "intoxicated with virtue," for the excitement he felt on observing the spectacle of urban vice distracted his attention from the unacceptable elements in his own character. In later years he was to marvel at his own perfect assurance while this exaltation lasted: "Nothing great or beautiful can enter the human heart of which I was not capable" (*O.c.*, I, 416). But the logic of the role he had elected forced him finally to quit the capital, and in his refuge at Mme d'Epinay's country house, where he retired with Thérèse and her mother in 1756, his elation abruptly collapsed. He fell into a kind of depressed torpor and was unable to continue the literary projects he had begun. In the quiet countryside the memory of his five abandoned children began to haunt him, and in order to protect himself from an overwhelming sense of guilt, he resolved to stop having sexual relations with Thérèse: "The remorse became so acute that it almost wrenched from me the public avowal of my crime at the beginning of *Emile*. I feared a repetition, and not wishing to run the risk I preferred to condemn myself to abstinence rather than expose Thérèse to being put in the same position again" (*O.c.*, I, 594–95).

Each measure Rousseau took to still the voices of accusation only plunged him deeper into his misery. Thérèse was offended by his withdrawal, leaving him still more isolated. Bound to a woman he could not love and to a personage he could not become, he felt his future was closing down before his very eyes. To find relief from a life rendered more and more unhappy by guilt and sexual frustration, he had recourse to a pastime that had occupied him often before his "intellectual and moral reform": the weaving of onanistic fantasies. He

turned to his past, recollecting and re-experiencing the pleasures he had known with women in his youth.

The imaginary return to an era predating his incarnation as
the "sage of Europe" unloosed a flood of memory, and once
more he was seized with elation. "Forgetting the human race
altogether," he related in the Confessions, "I made myself
societies of perfect beings, as celestial by their virtue as their
beauty, sure, tender, and faithful friends, such as I never
found here below" (O.c., I, 427–28). In his mind the "society of
perfect beings" slowly crystallized into two lovely young cous-
ins, Julie and Claire, and their tender tutor, Saint-Preux. The
central daydream of La Nouvelle Héloïse, of the virtuous lovers who live together but may neither yield to their passion
nor overcome it, began to take shape in Rousseau's mind.

A fervent desire for greater involvement led him one step
further. To experience his dream world more intensely, he
alternately imagined himself to be Julie, Claire, and Saint-
Preux, writing letters that depicted the different emotions these
changing roles aroused in him. Then he copied the letters on
beautiful gilt-edged paper, sprinkling azure and silver powder
to dry the ink, so that later he could open and read them, his
heart beating "with as much delight as if he had received them
from a beloved mistress." [16] In this way Rousseau was able to
imagine emanations of himself as distinct personalities: to
feel, as Saint-Preux, overwhelming desire for himself as Julie;
to feel, as Julie, passionate love for himself as Saint-Preux.
Over and over he objectified his characters and then remerged
with them in an illusion so successful that he was intoxicated
with "torrents of the most delicious feelings that have ever
entered a human heart" (O.c., I, 427).

For Rousseau, however, "delicious sentiments" were those
he felt in situations of intense erotic arousal, not those accom-
panying actual sexual intercourse. On the contrary, the moment of possessing a woman was invariably disappointing to

him. What he said of his adventure with Zulietta, the beautiful Venetian courtesan, could apply to every liaison he had: "I deadened all the delights, I killed them as if at will" (*O.c.*, I, 320). Rousseau found his pleasure in masturbating while dreaming about situations of protracted sexual tension. In the daydream which became *La Nouvelle Héloïse* he simultaneously created the situation he most enjoyed, one where desire could neither be satisfied nor diminished, and the means for enjoying it, the writing of letters which he sent and received. The fantasy of Julie, Saint-Preux, and Claire permitted him to forget the failures of his own life—the abandoned children, the chains of dependency binding him at once to Thérèse and to sexual abstinence, and the seeming dead end of his ambitions to play a role in the world. He created a paradise where, as each character in turn, he was not only free from remorse but so innocent that his innermost thoughts and feelings were open to the scrutiny of others. The unique value of the novel, he said in the *Confessions*, lay in the fact that it was "a book with no wickedness of any kind, neither in the characters nor in the actions" (*O.c.*, I, 546).

Rousseau's response to the conflicts aroused in him by the disparity between his private life and his public image was to deny the meaning of the former. He attempted to insulate himself in a personal world where intentions, not actions, were the sole measure of virtue. When Diderot wrote to him in 1757, warning "woe unto him who lives and has no duty of which he is the slave" (*C.*, I, 235), Rousseau became enraged at his friend's failure to acknowledge the purity of his feelings. "Ingrate," he answered, "I never did you any favors, but I loved you; and you will never in your life repay me for what I have felt for you" (*C.*, I, 243).

The quarrel became public, as it was bound to, when Rousseau singled out the statement in *Le Fils naturel* that "only the wicked man is alone" and insisted on viewing it as a personal indictment. The remark appears in the context of a long development in which Diderot emphasizes the primacy of the social order, condemning the man who refuses to become a husband and father. It was a passage that, Rousseau thought, was intended deliberately to provoke him: "In our altercations you have always been the aggressor. I am sure I never did you any harm other than not enduring patiently enough the harm you liked to do me, and there I admit I was wrong. I was happy in my solitude; you took it upon yourself to trouble my happiness and you did a good job of it. Besides, you said that only the wicked man is alone, and to justify your sentence you must, at any price, see to it that I become wicked" (*C.*, I, 237).

In his dialogue *Rousseau juge de Jean-Jacques*, a book which he wrote in 1776, wrapped in a paper addressed to God, and attempted to lay on the great altar at Notre-Dame, Rousseau returned to Diderot's sentence of almost twenty years before, bitterly denouncing his former friend's injustice:

The timid, weak man who has no courage and who tries to remain on the sidelines for fear of being cast down and trod under the feet of the crowd is therefore wicked, according to you, the others who are stronger, harder, more ardent to pierce are the good ones? I saw this doctrine for the first time in a discourse published by the *philosophe* Diderot precisely at the time when his friend J.-J. had retired into solitude. "Only the wicked," he said, "are alone." Until then, people had regarded the love of solitude as one of the least equivocal signs of a peaceful and healthy soul, free from ambition, envy, and all the burning passions born of egoism which are produced and fermented in society. The really sociable man is more difficult in his relationships than others, those which consist only of false appearances cannot suit him. He would rather live far from the wicked without thinking about them than to see them and hate them. This is how J.-J. had to think and behave before the conspiracy of which he was the object; judge for yourself if now that it exists and extends its traps all around him, he must find pleasure in living with his persecutors, in seeing himself the object of their derision, the plaything of their hatred, the dupe of their perfidious caresses [etc.]. (*O.c.*, I, 789–90)

While Rousseau was trying to protect his self-esteem by curling up inside himself at the country estates of his rich protectors, Diderot was feeling more and more beset and isolated in Paris. Attacks against the *Encyclopédie* mounted to the point where d'Alembert resigned from his editorship, and all Diderot's friends urged him to do the same. Voltaire, by means of some private logic, said that Diderot was "unworthy of the name philosopher," that he was "cowardly" for not abandoning the enterprise when d'Alembert did.[17] But Diderot clung defiantly to the editorship as he did to his role as pater familias. He continued to fulfill, however poorly, his functions as Antoinette's husband and Angélique's father, although he scarcely had a good word to say for either of them.

His theoretical enthusiasm for the father's role seemed to wax as the pleasures of his domestic life waned. In *Le Fils naturel*, immediately after Constance proclaims that "in order to be happy, one must have the approbation of one's own heart, and perhaps that of other men. You will not obtain either, if you quit the post marked out for you," she introduces a long discourse on the moral obligation of raising one's own children, insisting on the parents' duty to supervise the upbringing of their offspring. "[Your children] will pass the first years of their lives under your eyes. That is enough to answer for the years which follow" (*A.-T.*, VII, 67). The play comes to a triumphant finale with the father's prayer: " 'May Heaven, which blesses the children through the parents, and the parents through the children, accord you ones who will resemble you, and who will render you the tenderness you have for me' " (*A.-T.*, VII, 84). In the same vein, the dedicatory preface of *Le Père de famille* consisted of a systematic exposé of parents' duties in educating their children.

This statement of solidarity with the social order and the validity of the obligations it imposed on its members revealed the growing antagonism between Rousseau and Diderot. For Rousseau, the inference of culpability cast upon the man who refused to fulfill his paternal obligations was tantamount to the supreme betrayal. Having opted for the inner experience of virtue, regardless of the psychic cost of pretending that reality did not exist, he found his friend's allegiance to the significance of action insufferable.

If Diderot had cut to the very quick of his friend's shame, Rousseau, in return, knew exactly where to direct the answering blow. "I do not at all believe . . . that one can be virtuous without religion," he remarked in a note to *La Lettre à d'Alembert sur les spectacles* (a pamphlet on the evils of the theater), ironically echoing Diderot's hypocritical dedication of Shaftesbury's *Inquiry.* "I long held that deceptive opinion of which I am only too disabused." [18] Until the end of his life Diderot preserved this remark in a list of "Rousseau's seven villainies." For him, the sevenfold villain had become "false, vain as Satan, ungrateful, a cruel hypocrite, and wicked." [19] By denying that it was possible to "have probity without religion," Rousseau was publicly negating the secret premise of Diderot's life: that he could be as good a man as his father without being pious like his brother. Diderot was as baffled as he was wounded by his friend's behavior because he could not reconcile Rousseau's protestations of virtue with the cruelty of his attack, nor could he understand the nature of his own provocations. "Is it then possible to be eloquent and sensitive without having principles of honor, or true friendship, or virtue, or truthfulness? That makes me angry," he wrote to his new mistress, Sophie Volland, describing his reaction to the *Lettre à d'Alembert* (*C.,* II, 145). He had difficulty recognizing the existence of a coherent personality in others as well as in himself; he attempted to equate the inner self with facile outer manifestations of sympathy and was endlessly pained by the discrepancies he discovered. His disappointment at his own inability to understand Rousseau, as well as his sensation of having been betrayed, made him cling to Sophie as to a guarantor of his integrity, for, after all, if Rousseau was not the "honest man" Diderot believed, could he be sure that his own virtue was what it seemed to be?

"I have erected a statue in her heart," he wrote of Sophie later in the same letter to her, "which I would never wish to be broken. What grief for her if I made myself guilty of an action lowering me in her eyes! Is it not true that you would like me better dead than wicked?" Sophie's real opinion of Diderot and her view of their relationship will probably never be known, since the letters she wrote appear to have been destroyed, but her role in his life was much as he delineated it. Where Mme de Puisieux had been his accomplice in delinquency, Sophie was the keeper of an icon, exerting her influence to help Diderot become consubstantial with the ideal model he had constructed of himself.

There are three mysteries surrounding Sophie Volland. The first one concerns her ambiguous role in her own family. Forty years old when she first met Diderot in 1757, the spinster daughter of a rich government official, she seems to have been kept on unusually short tether by her widowed mother. It was taken for granted that Sophie was in some way indentured for life to the redoubtable Mme Volland, who shuttled her daughter back and forth from their country house at Isle to their home in Paris like a trunk or a pet. Diderot's biographers have speculated that perhaps she had never married and was treated so peremptorily because of some scandal in her past.[20] Her mother's conduct toward her would be more easily explainable if Sophie had, at some point, strayed from the strict decorum demanded of the unmarried daughter of a rich family. In any case, Sophie's unquestioning compliance with her mother's least whim was a source of constant frustration for Diderot, who found himself obliged to observe the greatest circumspection even to be able to correspond with her.

If her relations with her mother were peculiar, her affection for her younger sister was more so. Mme Le Gendre, married to an engineer, flirting with any man she met, apparently expressed her true sexual preferences best in her sister's arms. There is little doubt that Sophie was the passive partner in an incestuous lesbian couple, one which Diderot tried in vain to disrupt.

The third mystery revolves around Diderot himself: of all the women available to him in Paris, why did he choose to fall deeply in love with a fortyish, mother-ridden, lesbian spinster sequestered six months out of every twelve in the country? It may have been that Sophie offered the best possible compromise between having a mistress and not having one. His early letters to her were a perennial courtship; she was always to be wooed, and won, it seems, only provisionally and intermittently. The situation brought out the best in Diderot; during her half-yearly sojourns at Isle he wrote her the loveliest and most intimate letters imaginable. It is in large measure from this correspondence, which served him in some ways as a journal, that we have a picture of Diderot's day-to-day life.

She must have seemed to him, above all, a *nice* woman, nice in the sense of being good-humored and of belonging to a more gracious milieu. As Sophie's lover, whatever rewards that position did or did not bring him on a given day, Diderot moved out of the quarrelsome lower-class farce he lived in with his wife, to inhabit a world of larger sentiments and more ample means. Sophie read philosophy through her "little spectacles," and however excessively bound to her family she may have been at times, she never shouted or threw pots, as Diderot's wife was wont to do.[21]

Unlike Rousseau, who regarded his friends with increasing suspicion, Diderot clung with desperate tenacity to those he had at once elected his judges and invested with his own desired virtue. "The three beautiful souls—yours, mine, and [Grimm's]!" he exclaimed in a letter to his mistress in June 1759 (C., II, 146). While Sophie's character has always remained a subject of conjecture (leaving aside her Sapphic relations with her sister), it is safe to presume that no one besides Diderot ever dreamed of calling the icily opportunistic Grimm a "beautiful soul." "If I were to lose one of the other two, who would fill this terrible void? Live, both of you, if you do not wish me to be one day the voice crying in the wilderness." His passionate attachment to Grimm curiously echoed his feeling for Sophie; it was dogged and often unreciprocated. He attributed the faithfulness and tenderness which he wished to perceive in himself to his friend and to his mistress and then treated them as if they displayed these qualities. He told Sophie of his reunion with Grimm after a separation of some weeks: "I could not unclench my teeth, either to eat or talk. He was beside me. I held his hand and looked at him. They treated us like a lover and his mistress toward whom one should be tactful" (C., II, 268). Many years later he wrote to Grimm, describing his feelings for him in terms strongly reminiscent of those employed by Rousseau's Saint-Preux in speaking to his beloved Julie in La Nouvelle Héloïse: "I feel myself bound to you so powerfully that I have never separated your actions from mine; that it is impossible for me to experience the least gratitude for favors; that, whatever you thought, you said, you did, it is I who says, who thinks, and who does. For twenty years I have believed myself to exist in two people" (C., XII, 63). Whereas Rousseau's need to create perfect beings endowed with his imaginary virtues led him to reject real people, a similar need in Diderot found expression in his purblind infatuation with Sophie and Grimm.

It was partly as a result of his anxious fixation on Sophie that Diderot began to perceive the flaw in his own virtue, a perception which was eventually to alter the very structures of his thought. In the summer of 1759 his father fell ill and was thought to be dying. Diderot, the champion of paternity, its rights and obligations, the author of *Le Fils naturel* and *Le Père de famille,* could not tear himself from his mistress's side to visit his father, even though he believed it could save his life if he went. It is interesting that instead of doing what Rousseau habitually did in such quandaries, that is, either deny his dereliction or attribute it to a corrupt society, he fell into a state of morose passivity. "His consultation [Dr. Tronchin's] would save my father, if I were there to see it executed," he wrote to Grimm, "but, my friend, I am a bad son. I cannot pull myself away from here" (*C.,* II, 129).

His father's death depressed him deeply, accompanied as it was by feelings of moral failure and impotence. He was haunted by his father's presence and tried to exorcise his image by incorporating it into Sophie's; as if to infuse it with the more flattering sensations he associated with her. "You will soften the idea I have of him," he told her. "It will not leave me even when I am close to you; but the touching and melancholy part of it, melting into the impressions of tenderness and sensuality that I get from you, there will come from this mélange of sentiments an altogether delicious state. Ah! If it could become habitual! It is only a question of being a good lover and a good son" (*C.,* II, 158). Whether or not Diderot considered himself a good lover, he was not satisfied that he had been a good son. "Now that the wings of youth no longer carry me in the air, over the surface of the earth, I am heavy, I am enervated" (*C.,* II, 176). He felt suffocated, as if the evidence of his deficiencies were palpable, and oppressed by a sense of his own inadequacies and by his need to be considered as good a man as his father had been. "Oh my friend," he told Sophie, "what a task my father has imposed upon me, if I ever wish to merit the honor paid to his memory" (C., II, 195). "When I walk down the street," he wrote to Grimm, "I hear the people who look at me say: 'It's the father himself.' I know there's nothing to it, and that, no matter what I do, there never will be anything to it" (C., II, 213).

Still, he resolved to behave as if he were as good a man as his father had been, beginning with the division of the estate. Imitating his ideal distinterested philosopher, he arranged the distribution in such a way as to give himself what he believed was the smallest portion.[22] He hoped that his family would admire such fidelity to the model he had constituted of a generous philosopher, and that admiration was more valuable to him than his inheritance. He returned to Paris from Langres encouraged by the impressions he felt he had made on his brother and sister. "I left them enchanted with me—them and everybody who had any part in our affairs. They are of one voice on the matter and I cannot hide the joy I feel" (C., II, 222).

In attempting to obey the imperative expressed in his father's last words, "Live in union," and to procure his brother's approval, Diderot had made a concession of far greater consequence than his rightful share of the estate. He promised Didier that he would never again publish a word against religion. The existence of this promise is revealed by two documents, one a memoir written by Abbé Didier in 1763 in which he enumerates his grievances against the philosopher: "My brother has no religion and is proud of not having any. My brother had promised me not to talk or write against religion. He did not keep his word" (C., IV, 243). Didier was apparently convinced that his brother was the author of De l'esprit and other freethinking works often attributed to him. But not until 1772 did Diderot finally conclude that Didier was irrevocably obdurate, that efforts at appeasement were futile, and that the time had come to withdraw his promise. The second document is the last letter Diderot ever wrote to Didier, in which he said: "Let us attempt to understand one another. I had a brother on whose friendship I was able to count by fulfilling certain conditions stipulated between us. I have rigorously fulfilled those conditions. Nonetheless, I have lost my brother. Hence, all pacts between us are null and void, and I am the master to do as I please, without him having any reason to complain" (C., XII, 133).

It was during those years between 1759 and 1772 that Diderot produced the works which future generations were to hail as his masterpieces. *La Religieuse, Le Neveu de Rameau, Le Rêve de d'Alembert,* and *Jacques le fataliste* were written in the privacy of his study, intended with few exceptions for Diderot's eyes alone, and free from the exigency of presenting an ideal philosopher who would at once impress the public and offer the author a model whom he could call himself. If, as Diderot remarks in *Le Neveu de Rameau,* his thoughts were his harlots, he had decided to enjoy their company unhampered by the petticoats of polite society. The promise to Didier marked the end of an era in Diderot's life and the beginning of a long and painful period of turning inward.

3/Bad Times

In the years following his father's death, Diderot felt alone
and abandoned, haunted by his father's absence and disappointed in his relations with his family and friends. He was
attempting to write plays, one of which, *Le Juge de Kent,*
had as its central character an awesome old man referred to
simply as "the judge." [1] But he found it difficult to work, and
the memory of his father constantly interposed itself between
his imagination and the page. "My mind wanders and it is no
longer the Judge of Kent whom I see but the cutlery maker of
Langres" (*C.,* II, 172), he wrote to Melchior Grimm. His domestic life had degenerated into sheer misery; Antoinette's
scenes had provoked him to the point of visiting her confessor
and threatening to "send her back to the poverty where [I]
found her" (*C.,* II, 124) if she did not mend her ways. Nor
did his mistress appear to provide much solace. His letters to
Sophie Volland from this period show a Diderot frantic and
jealous, aware of her lesbian relations with her sister and yet
incapable of effective opposition. "Do you forget me in the
tumult of parties and in your sister's arms?" he asked, and then,
addressing himself to Mme Le Gendre, he pleaded: "take care
of her health and remember that pleasure also exacts a price"

(*C.*, III, 69). "Why have you abandoned me?" he asked Sophie. "Melancholy found my soul unguarded."

It was becoming difficult to ignore Grimm's growing sympathy with the mentality of his royal patrons, although Diderot did the best he could, continuing to give his friend the benefit of every doubt. Finally Mme d'Epinay, Grimm's mistress, complained to him of her lover's cynicism. "He [Grimm] is losing the severity of his principles," Diderot told Sophie. "I see all this as well as she; however, I excuse him as best I can" (*C.*, III, 267).

He clung to his conviction that human nature was essentially good and that moral evil must result from forces alien to man's character. Like Rousseau, he needed to experience his own virtue and at the same time find an explanation for his own morally unacceptable acts. But, unlike Rousseau, who carried the syllogism of self-justification to its logical conclusion by leaving society, Diderot could not face the prospect of living alone. To Sophie he described the intellectual and personal morass into which his conflicting desires had led him. "No, dear friend, nature had not made us wicked; it is bad education, bad examples, and bad legislation which has corrupted us. If that is an error, at least it is one which I am happy to find in my own heart, and I would be very sorry if experience or reflection were ever to undeceive me. What would become of me? I would have either to live alone, or believe that I was ceaselessly surrounded by wicked people, and neither possibility suits me." [2]

He was desperately concerned that his group, the *philosophes*, should appear to the outside world as above reproach.[3] He worried about his friends' morals, fearing that some unedifying episode would become known to the general public and give the gossips material for slandering them. "It is not enough to know more than they do," he wrote to Voltaire, "it must be shown that we are better than they are and that philosophy makes more good people than grace, sufficient or efficacious. They would like it, the perverse creatures, if I authorized them to denounce our sentiments by some bad act, but by God! I will not" (C., IV, 177). Love affairs, because they were based on natural inclination and free from the superstitious trappings surrounding legalized marriage, were acceptable in Diderot's eyes, but for him this was all the more reason to conduct them on the loftiest moral level. If an extramarital liaison was in keeping with philosophy, dalliance was anathema. He fretted about the possibility of philandering among his friends Grimm, Mme d'Epinay, the Baron d'Holbach, and his wife. "See what the wretches who surround us and spy on us will say about it," he fumed to Sophie. "It would be nothing for them, but what a crime they would make of it for us, whom they hate to acknowledge as virtuous people. Can't you just hear them: 'Well now! These philosophers, so that's what they're like. etc.'" (C., IV, 45).

He continued to feel hurt and rejected by his brother, who in spite of promises and gestures of reconciliation still refused to see him as anything other than a hardened sinner. His sister, an amenable creature, all too often seemed to take the Abbé's side. "If things go on like this I shall go home, sell my patrimony, and forget people who do not deserve a brother like me," he grumbled. But the thought of a permanent rupture with those he loved filled him with dismay. "Forget them? I don't know what I am saying. I would never be able to" (C., III, 270).

In spite of his theoretical enthusiasm for fatherhood, he still showed little interest in his daughter, Angélique, and blamed his wife for so mishandling the girl that she had become incorrigibly mediocre. "She shows an aptitude for all physical and mental exercises. [Mme Le Gendre] or her sister would have turned her into a surprising individual, and her mother, who has gotten hold of her, will never permit me to make anything of her at all. Oh well! She will resemble a hundred thousand others" (*C.*, III, 300).

He faced each situation with the same sort of despairing passivity, blustering or pleading with his wife, his mistress, and his friends, but seemingly unable to influence their behavior in any decisive way, as if his fear of isolation had reduced him to immobility. It was in this mood of near-frozen panic that he became involved in the plot to deceive his friend the Marquis de Croismare.

It was the summer of 1760; Diderot's friends were leaving Paris as usual for more agreeable parts, and he was left with an even heavier burden of responsibility than that which he bore during the year. In the spring M. de Croismare, a member of the *philosophes'* circle, had decided to quit Paris for his estate in Normandy. As time went on it became apparent that he did not intend to return, for he had discovered the consolations of religion. Few circumstances in life were harder for Diderot to bear than being abandoned by a friend; as we have seen, it was Rousseau's retirement from society which most infuriated him, and to be left in favor of religion poured salt on the wound. It so happened that M. de Croismare, a high-minded and tender-hearted gentleman, had, a few years earlier, become passionately interested in accounts of the efforts of a young nun, Marguérite de la Marre, to be released from her religious vows, which in the eighteenth century were civil vows as well, and, without ever having seen her, had enlisted himself in her cause. Her plea was nonetheless rejected and she was sent back to the convent. Now, Diderot, Grimm, and certain other members of the group mounted an eccentric cabal with the avowed purpose of enticing their friend to return to Paris. A series of letters purporting to be from the nun was drafted and sent to the unsuspecting Marquis by Diderot and his friends. In the letters the "nun" told M. de Croismare that she had heard of his interest in her cause and begged him for his help now that she had escaped from the convent and was in hiding. So innocent was the Marquis and so artful were the *philosophes* that their victim was totally deceived by the forged correspondence. He became enthralled with the prospect of serving the unfortunate "Sister Suzanne" to the point of offering her asylum at his château in Normandy. But since the point of the hoax had been to induce him to return to Paris, the *philosophes* decided regretfully to end the matter by informing him of Sister Suzanne's demise.

Diderot, however, became so engrossed in his role as the renegade nun that he resolved to write a sort of memoir or autobiographical letter which would detail her plight in such a way as to disarm the Marquis completely. The memoir-writing assumed a life of its own, and it was eventually this manuscript which took the form of the novel, *La Religieuse*, published twenty years later in the *Correspondance littéraire*.[4]

La Religieuse was engendered by a set of circumstances in Diderot's life analogous to those which had led Rousseau to write *La Nouvelle Héloïse*. Both men had reached a kind of stalemate in their literary careers, the result of conflicts between the need to feel virtuous and the exigencies of reality. Both felt especially impelled toward filling an emotional void left by their dissatisfaction with the intimate associations of their own lives.[5] For Rousseau the solution lay in disengaging himself as much as possible from real people and in projecting alter egos like the letter-writing Julie, Saint-Preux, and Claire, in order to experience his own fantasies more intensely.

The impetus behind *La Religieuse* was not toward severing links with real people, but, on the contrary, toward strengthening them. If Diderot had been hurt by M. de Croismare's defection, he did not respond by turning away from him but rather by trying to bring him closer. *La Religieuse*, at the time of its completion in 1761, was from the first page to the last an effort at seduction. Diderot, in this reprehensible prank, was not preoccupied with his image as the virtuous *philosophe,* and he was able to demonstrate a keen intuitive understanding of his friend. M. de Croismare, a widower, was lonely on his estate in Normandy and was attempting to assuage his need for companionship with religion. Sister Suzanne was created to ignite the imagination of the isolated Marquis, whose daydreams were no mystery to Diderot and his friends. Several years before, he had commissioned an artist, M. Mengs, to do two pastels for him according to the following descriptions reported in the *Correspondance littéraire:*

First picture: A woman with a lovely face, nobly coquettish, seductively dressed; she should wear few ornaments but their effect should be piquant. She should let part of her bosom be seen and one should glimpse an interesting body form. She should let her glance drop tenderly on a philosopher who should be [the subject of the second picture].

Second picture: A man of an age when the graces have acquired some consistency. He should be dressed in classical style, with the attributes of philosophy. His garments will permit some beautiful nude part of him to be seen. He should seem tenderly distracted by the sight of the charming intruder. He should regard the frivolous woman with embarrassment and a kind of shame, wanting to see her and fearing to be seen. (*C.l.,* II, 38–39)

As Diderot has Suzanne depict herself, she is a most appealing creature. She reports the homage paid to her beauty, her charm, and her intelligence in an innocent way suggesting that she is unaware of her personal attraction. In the first paragraph of the novel she tells the Marquis, "I certainly was worth more than my sisters, judging by the charms of my mind and my face, my character and my talents" (*O.r.,* 236). A young man courting her sister quickly comes to prefer her, and continues his suit only as a pretext to be in her presence. When she sings and accompanies herself on the clavichord at the convent at Longchamps, she comments, "I do not know what effect it produced; but they did not listen to me for long, they interrupted me with compliments" (*O.r.*, 257). The most evocative scenes, however, those making the most direct appeal to M. de Croismare's pity and sensuality, are presented without commentary. In the dim chapel where she kneels to ask forgiveness for her sins, she is stripped to the waist, her thick hair pushed to one side of her neck. Her superior at Saint Eutrope takes off her veil and her wimple, fixes her hair, and undresses her. In her despair, Suzanne tears at her clothing; the mad nun at Longchamps rips off her habit; and the lesbian Mother Superior at Saint Eutrope in her final delirium runs nude through the corridors. These vivid tableaux create an atmosphere of sensuality which reaches its climax in an attempted seduction of Suzanne by her superior.

The Marquis de Croismare, however wavering as he may be between philosophy and religion, was not to be captivated by the senses alone. Sister Suzanne possesses a character as exemplary as her person is enticing. Diderot presented her as a kind of Clarissa, differing from Richardson's heroine only in the important respect that she had not contributed to her own downfall. Her burden of misfortunes results from the combined depravity of social institutions and the hypocritical practices of convent life. "The more I think about it," she remarks, "the more I am persuaded that what is happening to me has never yet happened and perhaps never will. At one moment (and God willing, the first and the last!), Providence, whose ways are unknown to us, has chosen to heap on one sole miserable being the whole mass of . . . [cruelties of convent life]" (*O.r.*, 307). Diderot, in the guise of Providence, had her endure her tribulations with admirable Christian forbearance, as when she protests, "I would not wish to have harmed a single hair on the head of my cruelest enemy" (*O.r.*, 347). This combination of suffering and humility is accompanied by an almost unbelievable innocence, which, says her confessor, Father Lemoine, could only have been brought about by a special attention from Providence. But her virtue, although inordinately well developed and miraculously preserved, is of a very special kind, drawn to measure for a gentleman *philosophe*. Like Candide or Fielding's Parson Adams, she must defend her Christian conscience (as envisaged by the unbelieving Diderot) against the Christian Church.

Thirteen years earlier, in *Les Bijoux indiscrets*, Diderot had elaborated the conceit that women, no matter how virtuous their appearance, were really motivated by extreme prurience; now Suzanne is shown to be totally devoid of sexual feeling. So chaste is her mind that she cannot understand the nature of her Mother Superior's advances, and even after having been enlightened, promptly forgets, reverting to her original bewilderment. Lest the Marquis be discouraged by such perhaps excessive innocence, however, she assures him that she is not by nature unloving: "I was born affectionate and I like being caressed" (*O.r.*, 371).

If in his own life Diderot found himself passive and powerless, trapped inside the "statue" of the philosopher he had assembled, he found a great source of energy in writing *La Religieuse*, a work intended to do something to someone else. The new set of circumstances seemed to free long pent-up powers. He had written to Mme d'Epinay regarding his adaptation of Edward Moore's *The Gamester* (a play in the same serious moral vein as his own works for the theater) that she and Grimm should do with it as they saw fit and "do nothing if it were not worth doing anything with," because he felt the writing was "uneven, diffuse, obscure, barbarous, and crabbed," but, on the other hand, *La Religieuse* swept him up and seemed to carry him along with it. "I am after my Nun," he wrote Damilaville, "but [the book] stretches out under my pen and I no longer know when I will touch the shore" (*C.*, III, 40). Several months later he wrote to Mme d'Epinay: "I go like the wind. It is no longer a letter, but a book. There will be true things in it, pathetic ones, and there could be strong things but I don't allow myself enough time. I let my mind go; anyway I could scarcely control it" (*C.*, III, 221).

The source of this unusual energy in writing *La Religieuse* lay in the free expression of desires he could not satisfy in either his public works or his private life. Failing to persuade Sophie or Grimm to stay by his side during the summer of 1760, he had directed his attentions to manipulating M. de Croismare. Instead of being an idealized but unsuccessful philosopher, middle-aged and unloved, he became the animator of an equally arbitrary personage, Sister Suzanne. In real life and in his works for publication he had felt bound to an identity that offered at best a compromise between his aspirations and his achievements, but in creating Sister Suzanne he was free to invest her with all his personal ideals and none of his defects. Through her he was able to do to M. de Croismare what he could not do to his mistress or his friend: fire the imagination to the point of controlling behavior. While Sophie and Grimm showed no inclination to alter their summer plans to satisfy Diderot's need for their presence, the Marquis was prepared to offer Suzanne a lifelong place at his side.

La Religieuse satisfied another aspect of Diderot's desire to become the active agent rather than the passive spectator. Georges May has pointed out that while Diderot was suspicious and jealous of Sophie's relations with Mme Le Gendre, it is not at all clear of which woman he was the more jealous. His letters to Sophie were meant to be read by her sister as well; they were sprinkled with seductive flattery of Mme Le Gendre and complaints that she was scornful of the entire male sex. It is difficult to determine whether he was more troubled by her ascendancy over Sophie or her rejection of him. "In vain I malign your sister," he wrote to Sophie, "the malice must all be on my tongue with none at all in my heart, for I realize that it is for her that I write all this. No, Madame, I hate you, I don't want to talk to you any more. What do you care, I am a man and you have contempt for us all" (*C.*, III, 74). But in writing *La Religieuse* this unpleasant situation was reversed. Diderot graphically described scenes of seduction which excluded the male, and it was M. de Croismare who was troubled and deceived. In real life Diderot was reduced to pleading with Sophie for reassurance: "I have become so extravagant, so unjust, so jealous; you speak so highly [of Mme Le Gendre], you become so impatient at the least criticism of her . . . I dare not finish! I am ashamed of what is going on inside me but I cannot help myself. Adieu. I am mad. How could I fail to be?" (*C.*, III, 74–75). But in composing Sister Suzanne's *apologia,* he was the master elaborating his fantasies of homosexual seduction, with M. de Croismare as the frustrated bystander.

He had promised his brother not to write against religion, and indeed he observed a careful distinction in the novel between "true piety" and "superstition, bigotry, and fanaticism." Nevertheless, the work, which he did not intend to publish, permitted him to give full vent to his favorite criticism of Didier: his election of the celibate state. Diderot's sexual bohemianism as a young man, his impetuous marriage, his affair with Sophie, had all called forth moralistic fulminations from Didier, who took great pride in the spotless purity of his own life. This pretension of moral superiority based on sexual abstinence infuriated Diderot, who wished to defend desire as both natural and socially useful. In *La Religieuse* Diderot depicted celibacy as an extravagant perversion, both dangerous to the individual and harmful to society. Since, in his view, it was impossible to stifle sexuality altogether, efforts to do so resulted at best in abuses like homosexuality and onanism, at worst in madness and death. "All the lugubrious ceremonies observed when the habit is taken, when a man or a woman is consecrated to monastic life and to misery, do they suspend the animal functions? On the contrary, do they not awaken in the silence, in the constraint, in the inactivity, with a violence unknown in society? Where does one find minds obsessed by impure specters, following and disturbing them?" (*O.r.*, 310).

Having expressed his opinion of Didier's claims for chastity, Diderot went on to the even more serious charge: Didier, with his airs of moral superiority, had failed to produce children, whereas Diderot, considered the disgrace of the family, had done as their father had, and founded a family. Fathering children, rearing them, had become a kind of theoretical *raison d'être* for Diderot. "To take a vow of chastity is to promise God the constant infraction of the wisest and most important of his laws" (*O.r.*, 311). "Yes, M. l'Abbé," he wrote to his brother at the time of their final rupture, "it is passion and desire, it is a natural attraction to which children owe their existence. It is by education and the pains they take that parents have the right to their children's respect and gratitude" (*C.*, XII, 162).

Diderot came a step closer to defining himself through writing *La Religieuse*. In opposition to his celibate brother and to Jean-Jacques, he championed man's social instincts and responsibilities as embodying the real demands of nature. Ironically, at the moment when he was feeling the most ill-treated by the social matrix, he was most heatedly attacking the gratifications of the solipsist.

In 1760, while Diderot was composing the novel, he was convinced, like Rousseau, of the innate goodness of mankind. He believed that the function of the literary artist was to lead the public in the direction of its natural virtue in certain specific ways. The work of art should represent various ordeals of virtuous human beings, especially in the context of their family relationships, so as to foster identification with the morally good people and contempt for their persecutors. The pity and empathy experienced by the spectator at a play or by the reader of a novel would predispose him to behave morally in his real life. Thus the man of letters could work for the betterment of society. He posed the question in his *Discours de la poésie dramatique:* "Human nature is good?— Yes, my friend, and very good. It is not human nature which should be blamed but miserable convention, which perverts man. After all, what moves us like the story of a generous action? Where is the wretch who can listen coldly to the woes of a good man? What a boon it would be to mankind if all the representative arts proposed a common objective for themselves and were to vie with the laws to make us love virtue and hate vice!" (*O.e.,* 196). Diderot was in this morally uplifting frame of mind when he composed *La Religieuse,* in which the innocent Sister Suzanne suffers a life of the cruelest misfortunes, brought about by the corruptions of society.

The disparity between two of his motives in writing the novel—between his desire to seduce the public to virtue and to seduce M. de Croismare back to Paris—found expression in a pair of works written shortly after *La Religieuse.* The *Eloge de Richardson,* intended for public consumption, echoed the sentiments of the *Discours de la poésie dramatique.* The other, *Le Neveu de Rameau,* meant for no eyes but his own, revealed a certain dissatisfaction with his previous point of view. In the *Eloge de Richardson,* written in 1761 shortly after the English novelist's death, he proclaimed the efficacy of moral literature with such insistence as belied his uneasiness. "What is virtue? It is, no matter how one considers it, a sacrifice of the self. The self-sacrifice which one executes in the imagination is a preconceived disposition toward immolating oneself in reality" (*O.e.*, 31). He drew upon his own experiences as proof of the validity of his assertion. After reading Richardson's novel, he wrote, "How good I was! How just! How satisfied with myself! When I was finished reading I was like a man at the end of a day spent in doing good" (*O.e.*, 30). Art could make people feel the same sensations they would feel after actually behaving virtuously. By weeping over the misfortunes of the saintly Clarissa and venting righteous indignation at the misconduct of the villainous Lovelace, the reader could experience his own virtue in a pleasurable way.

For Diderot, "men are divided into two classes: those who enjoy and those who suffer" (*O.e.*, 33). The artist's function was to lead the reader to identify exclusively with the victim, and in that way, he would be conditioned, without even being aware of it, toward virtue. The artist, the character, and the reader should merge in an emotional union so powerful as to suspend all sense of incredulity, so that, "overwhelmed by grief or transported with joy, you will no longer have the strength to hold back your tears, and to say to yourself: 'But maybe that isn't true'" (*O.e.*, 35). Thus the novel would do for the worldly what the Bible did for the pious, provide virtue for those who accepted its words as literally true. Richardson's work, like the Bible, would serve to distinguish between those people susceptible to true moral enthusiasm and the hopelessly cynical. "I was comparing the work of Richardson to a book more sacred still, to a Gospel brought to the earth to separate the husband from the wife, the father from the son, the daughter from the mother, the brother from the sister" (*O.e.*, 38), said Diderot.

How closely allied these theories of emotional uplift through identification with suffering were to Diderot's feelings of failure and impotence may be judged by the last sentence of the *Eloge:* "While I converse with you [the characters in

Clarissa], the years for working and gathering laurels pass, and I advance toward the last term, without attempting anything which could recommend me to the times to come" (*O.e.*, 48).

The spring of 1761 found Diderot beginning ever so tentatively to question whether mankind was as fundamentally good as he had believed, and whether the art which moved men to tears really touched a source of unsullied virtue. His drama *Le Père de famille*, written in accord with the sentimental-aesthetic principles later outlined in the *Eloge*, had encountered severe opposition from the antiphilosophic cabal, even though these same critics had been observed weeping at performances of the play. He wrote to Voltaire in February 1761, asking questions which were to preoccupy him for many years to come. "Is it not incredible that men who can be moved to tears, are at the same time doing everything possible to denigrate the one who touches their feelings? Is the soul of man then but a dark cave, which virtue shares with the furies? If they weep, they are not wicked, but if, while they weep, they are suffering, wringing their hands, gritting their teeth, how can one imagine they are good?" (*C.*, III, 292).

Diderot had taken the doctrine that sensitivity was the outer manifestation of virtue to its logical extreme in *La Religieuse*, where the Mother Superior at Arpajon, enjoying a convulsive orgasm while embracing Sister Suzanne, is described as "good"—for after all, said Diderot, "it is impossible to be so sensitive without being good" (*O.r.*, 344). Now, however, doubts were beginning to present themselves. His experiences over the preceding years—the attacks against the *Encyclopédie*, his rupture with Rousseau, his suspicions about Grimm's principles and Sophie's predilections—were becoming increasingly difficult to reconcile with his effusions over the innate virtue of man. Yet in his works for publication he had locked himself into the position of the apologist of natural goodness. To Sophie he began to express his speculations about another aspect of human psychology—the possibility that we are all a bit tainted after all, and that even where we behave well, we enjoy the spectacle of vice from time to time to gratify our need for pleasures which are not virtuous. "Libertines are welcome in society, because we prefer vices which serve or amuse us to virtues that humiliate or sadden us; because they are full of indulgence for their faults, among which are some of ours . . . because they talk to us about what we dare neither mention nor do, because we are always a bit vicious. In a word, the libertine holds the place of libertinage which we deny ourselves" (*C.*, III, 30–31).

In *Le Neveu de Rameau,* an extremely unconventional work in dialogue form, written in 1761 and not intended for publication,[6] Diderot personified that libertine in the character Lui, giving him freedom to describe "that place of libertinage which we deny ourselves." Lui is endowed with exquisite taste in aesthetic matters but seems to be totally deprived of moral sense. The very idea of such a person contradicts the basis of Shaftesbury's theory that aesthetic taste and moral discernment were inextricably wed in the human soul. The Neveu is capable of a profound appreciation of the beautiful; to the good he is indifferent, and he professes a casual skepticism toward the whole question of the true. "When I pronounce the word 'song,' I have no clearer ideas than you and most of your ilk when you say reputation, blame, honor, vice, virtue [etc.]," he tells his interlocutor, Moi.

Having freed himself from the necessity of presenting an idealized *philosophe* before the world, Diderot permitted Lui to elaborate the full consequences of a consistently amoral attitude. In so doing Lui furnishes a critique of Shaftesbury's system of innate virtue finding expression in social relations.

Moi, the spokesman for Diderot's public philosophical position, is forced to the conclusion that his own beliefs are more beautiful but scarcely more rationally defensible than Lui's. "How is it," asks Moi, "that with such fine taste, such great sensitivity for the beauties of the musical art, you are so blind toward beautiful things in morals, so insensitive to the charms of virtue?" (*O.r.*, 473). Lui's answer illustrates Diderot's ambivalence concerning the respective roles of nature and society in forming the individual: perhaps Lui has a defective or missing fiber which renders him immune to moral beauty, or perhaps it is the fact that he has always "lived with good musicians and wicked people." Or maybe it is the "paternal molecule" that is to blame. In any case Lui wants to deny that he had had any choice in the matter. But Moi expresses doubts as to the inevitability of the Neveu's abject state, implying that if he understood the real nature of his interests, he would try to turn his talents to better account and earn, as an artist, the rewards he sought by living as a parasite of the rich. The Neveu protests that spending his days listening to the mindless chatter of his patrons has spoiled him "for the great things." "It would be better," Moi answers, "to lock oneself in an attic, drink water, eat dry bread, and try to find oneself" (*O.r.*, 482). But *why* would it? At this point, where Diderot needed to spell out the advantages of the virtuous life over the self-indulgent one, he seemed to hesitate and then retreat, as if he sensed the argument to be not only beyond his strength but perhaps beyond his conviction.

The *Encyclopédistes* in general and Diderot in particular enshrined Socrates as a founding saint of the philosophic life.[7] His martyrdom to truth at once replicated and countered the powerfully moving Christian tradition of martyrs to the Faith. For Diderot the identification with Socrates was especially personal and compelling. He dreamed of writing Socrates' life, "preceded by a discourse, the object of which would be to convince men that, all things considered, they have nothing better to do in this world than to practice virtue" (*C.*, II, 107). Although he often returned to the project he never wrote it, concerned, as he told Sophie, that if he failed it would be a hundred times worse than if he had never tried. In the Socratic dialogues, the thesis that virtue is always dependent on knowledge of what good and evil really are, that the immoral man is actually in error, mistaking the nature of his own interests, is given concrete epiphany in the dialogue form itself. Socrates elicits, he does not expound: the philosopher leads men toward the self-knowledge that will make them virtuous by means of a technique largely free from didactic exposition.

In *Le Neveu de Rameau*, Moi has the role of a wavering Socrates, convinced in his own mind of the necessity for virtue in the happy life, but afraid to put his belief to the test of the Neveu's adroit cynicism. When Lui states his view of the good education as being "that which leads to all sorts of pleasures without peril or inconvenience" (*O.r.*, 479), Moi wants to end further discussion by accepting that ambiguous formulation: "It would not take much for me to agree with you; but let us be careful not to pursue it."

"Why?" asks Lui.

"Because I fear that our agreement is only apparent and that if we once get into a discussion of the perils and inconveniences to be avoided, we would understand one another no more."

"What difference does that make?" asks the Neveu, apparently untroubled by the prospect of such a discussion.

"Let it be, I tell you," answers Moi (*O.r.*, 479).

Whereas in the Socratic dialogues the philosopher appeared as a kind of quirky gadfly, needling a pompous or rigid opponent, in *Le Neveu* these roles are reversed. It is Moi who is reduced to the uneasy self-protection of the established, while the Neveu seems to possess endless reserves of expansive energy and the flexibility of the uncommitted.

In Lui's description of the life he led as a lackey to the antiphilosophic clique, Diderot vented his spleen against it for its incessant persecutions of the *philosophes*. He showed its members as animals, racked with envy toward men of genius, devouring reputations "like starved wolves," and devoid of the faintest ethical sense.

But a disquieting shift takes place within the dialogue. The society of "Bertinhus," which the Neveu so scathingly satirizes, seems in many ways to mirror society at large. Convention coats the ferocity of human beings with the merest veneer; underneath is to be found Shaftesbury's concept of social interdependence turned inside out, each being seeking his pleasure at the expense of others. In that sense society, far from perverting man's true essence, is modeled upon it: "In nature all the species devour one another, all the ranks devour one another in society" (*O.r.*, 427). The Neveu differs from the ordinary run of men only in that he has dispensed with self-deception on a certain level, if not with self-justification. He acknowledges his viciousness although he attributes it indifferently to heredity, physiology, or the corruption of society. He gives voice to the things "that one thinks, that govern one's conduct, but that one does not say. In all truth that was the difference between my man and most of our circle. He admitted the vices he had, which others have, but he was not a hypocrite" (*O.r.*, 477). On the other hand, the Neveu is at least intellectually consistent in his admiration of great scoundrels, although he does not seem able to excel in that calling himself.

Diderot gave Lui his head to express his most daring speculations, and he could do so by making the separation between him and Moi very firm. Moi tolerates Lui now and then but in no way considers him an equal. Even though he can function as a bit of leavening in an otherwise stiflingly hypocritical world, Moi states emphatically: "I do not care for that kind of eccentric" (*O.r.*, 397). At the point where Lui forces the unwilling Moi to turn from the theoretical question of morality to the practical problem of how his daughter is to be raised, Moi registers a certain discomfort. He outlines a vague plan of studies based upon the society's ideals. Besides instruction in music she would have lessons in "grammar, mythology, history, geography, a little drawing, and a lot of morality" (*O.r.*, 421). The Neveu expostulates that such an education in "a world like ours" is useless and perhaps dangerous. The only meaningful training for a girl in society as it really functions is that which teaches her to be "pretty, amusing, and a flirt" (*O.r.*, 420).

The Neveu has known grief in his life. He counted on his wife's marvelously voluptuous rump to engage the profitable passion of "at least a farmer-general," but she died and, not only that, left him a son instead of a daughter, from whom he might have expected some advantage. The Neveu's point of view induces a powerful malaise in Moi—as if the panorama of human nature viewed head-on without the spectacles of Shaftesbury's optimism were too appalling to gaze upon for long. "I began to find it difficult tolerating the presence of a man who discusses a horrible act . . . as a connoisseur of painting or of poetry examines a work of art," Moi comments. "I became gloomy in spite of myself" (*O.r.*, 462). The Neveu personifies the frightening world of "natural" man, where each individual victimizes those less powerful and cringes before those more powerful than himself. From the lowliest servant to the King,"whoever needs someone else is indigent and strikes a pose. The King assumes a posture before his mistress and before God, he does his step in the vile pantomime. The minister does the step of the courtesan, the flatterer, the valet, or the beggar before the King. The ambitious throng dances your

positions in a hundred ways, one more vile than the next, before the minister. What you call the beggar's pantomime is
the great jog of the world" (*O.r.*, 487).

The only exception to this bitterly ironic picture is "one
being dispensed from the pantomime. That is the philosopher
who has nothing and asks nothing" (*O.r.*, 488). The role of
philosopher, which had at times seemed to Diderot so op-
pressively constraining, now offered a refuge from the revolt-
ing intercourse of the rest of mankind. As painful as it was,
"I want to die if it is not better than groveling, debasing, and
prostituting oneself" (*O.r.*, 489).

Repudiating society after investing it with all the impurities
one wishes to disavow was precisely the formula Rousseau
had discovered five years earlier, at the time of his "intellectual
and moral reform." Now, concealed by the privacy of his own
walls and his promise to his brother, Diderot tried the ascetic's
pose he had reviled Rousseau for striking. His model was not
the hermit crouching somewhere in a glade, but Diogenes,
rubbing mankind's collective nose in his indifference to their
existence.[8]

This state of self-publicized autonomy, however, although it
was immensely attractive to Diderot, bore little relation to
his real personality. In his own life he continued to need intimacy with the people he had elected to share his thoughts
and feelings.

4/The Project of Sincerity

Le Neveu de Rameau had reopened, in Diderot's mind, the whole question of the philosopher's role. The definition which Moi put forth in the dialogue would have logically led him to purchase a barrel and embark upon a Diogenean existence, but logic would have left him bereft of the supporting relations he needed. Instead, in the summer of 1762, he turned to Sophie, proposing a project which would at once bring them closer together and help him to become more virtuous. In their letters to one another, he told her, each would record

his every thought, every movement of his heart, all his pleasures, and all his troubles. One would need a great deal of courage in order to reveal everything, perhaps it would be easier to accuse oneself of planning a great crime than of a little, obscure, vile, base feeling. Perhaps it would cost less to write "I desired the throne at the expense of its occupant's life" than to write "one day when I was at the baths, among a great number of young people, I noticed one who was surprisingly beautiful, and I could not help approaching him." This kind of examination would not be without utility for oneself, either. I am sure that in the long run one would be anxious to have nothing but honest things to report. I would ask you: "Would you tell everything?" Ask your sister the same question, because it would be necessary to give up a project of sincerity which frightened you. For me, separated from you as I am, I know of nothing which would bring you closer to me than telling you everything and rendering you present at my actions by my accounting of them. (*C.*, IV, 39–40)

A project of sincerity: Diderot would reveal himself utterly before his mistress and her sister as well; they, in return, would render him privy to their most intimate thoughts and desires. Instead of "guarding the statue of the ideal philosopher," Sophie was invited to look at the man himself and be looked at by him. Although it would seem that Diderot wanted to be free of the yoke of the philosopher's role which he had borne so long and to offer Sophie the more spontaneous side of himself, at the same time, as the passage quoted above reveals, he hoped that in exploring himself before her, he would somehow become more worthy, more similar to his ideal.

During the months that followed, Diderot ventured confidences about his feelings for Grimm, who seemed to be going blind. Diderot became aware that his reaction to Grimm's illness was a kind of elation. His friend's misfortune would give him the opportunity to prove his own virtue: "The moment is coming when I will learn the worth of our protestations, our vows, our self-esteem, if I know how to be a friend. If I do not find *me,* how I shall scorn myself. If my friend goes blind, I call you as witness to my behavior. The sad moment for my friend! The great moment for me, if I am not mistaken" (*C.*, IV, 75).

He recounted to Sophie various small failures of his inner being to live up to his public image, ignoble motives, petty cowardices, unseemly lechery, pleading with her from time to time: "Love me in spite of everything I tell you!" (*C.*, IV, 78). Throughout their liaison he had insisted on his utter faithfulness to her, declaring that she was the only woman he desired. Now, in a letter of September 28, 1767, he began to question his motivation. Was his fidelity really based on the perfection of his love; was he, after all, the "new Céladon"? Or were there less admirable reasons for ignoring the advances of, for example, Sophie's elder sister, Mme de Blacy?

Before I erect a trophy to myself, I would have a hundred questions to ask. For example: "Was there not some principle of economy in your refusal? By any chance would you be afraid of having more asked of you than you have to give? Did you not prefer leaving a high opinion of yourself to enjoying a moment's satisfaction? The proverb: a beautiful watch but it does not keep time, did it pass vaguely through your mind?" Ah, dear friend, once one begins to analyze man's most heroic actions, one never knows how they will come out, and someone who thinks well of himself because of his actions would change his mind if he seriously tried to figure out the reasons. (*C.*, VII, 150)

The project of mutual confidences which was to assuage Diderot's loneliness and cement the bonds between him and his mistress had a paradoxical effect. Instead of deepening his intimacy with Sophie, the continual self-examination gradually brought a rift between them. As he studied the real motives underlying his attachment to her, he felt less impelled to convince himself of the idealized reasons. Little by little, in his letters to her through the years 1762 to 1767, his independence began to assert itself. By deflating the grandiose image he had constructed of himself, he seemed to need her approbation less. It was as if in coming to face the ignoble aspects of his own nature, the thirst for his mistress's approval were somehow slaked. His letters continued to be both frequent and affectionate, but the former tone of pleading to be admired gradually diminished. "If other people were as crabbed, unjust, sensitive, stormy, jealous, foolish, dumb, stupid, and werewolfish as I, there would be no way to get along" (C., IV, 187), he told Sophie in a letter in which, for the first time, he attempted to analyze his own responsibility for the unhappy state of his domestic life.

Revealing to Sophie and therefore to himself that he was frequently moved by mean or childish impulses did not eliminate those motivations, however, as he had hoped it would. Instead, he began to interpret other people's behavior in the light of his own experience, coming to the conclusion that if he was not especially good, others were no better. "Once one acquires the habit of reading one's own heart, one is well aware of what goes on in other people's. This assiduous examination of the self serves less to improve than to teach that neither oneself nor others are especially good" (C., V, 228).

He had slowly reversed the terms of the argument set forth in the *Essai sur le mérite,* and the position in which he now found himself was the antithesis of Shaftesbury's, in other words, something very close to Hobbes.[1] From seeing himself and all of mankind as essentially good, he had gone on, in *Le Neveu de Rameau,* to essay the point of view that only the philosopher was exempt from the law of ruthless egotism that ruled the rest of mankind. Now, after a period of extended introspection, he had concluded that the human race in general, including himself, was driven by a variety of motives, from the basest to the loftiest.

If the human soul were not a limpid source of virtue, however, which had somehow become polluted by contact with a dirty world, and were instead envisioned as an adaptive mechanism, devoted to two grand ends—"the preservation of the self and the propagation of the species" (C., IV, 85)—in what way could the artist or the philosopher possibly lead men to be better? In re-examining his theories of literature's moral effectiveness he rejected the optimism he had expressed in the *Eloge de Richardson.* Returning to the capital argument set forth in the *Eloge*—that the tears shed by the reader of a novel or the spectator at a play in which the innocent are persecuted were an involuntary manifestation of his morally excellent self, the very spontaneity of his sympathy guaranteeing its authenticity—Diderot now saw those same tears as a token of social hypocrisy, a device learned early in order to impress others with our goodness and at the same time allow us to experience ourselves in a flattering way. "Everything is . . . experimental in us," he said in his *Salon* of 1767. "The child learns early that politeness makes him agreeable to others and he lends himself to the charade. Later on in life he will discover that these exterior manifestations promise benevolence and humanity. We prefer hearing the story of a beautiful act to reading it alone. The tears it draws from us fall on the cold leaves of a book. They endear us to no one. We need live witnesses" (*A.-T.*, XI, 70). This is why plays produce such wonderful sensations of virtuous sympathy in the spectator's breast but do not lead, in reality, to his behaving any better. On the contrary, they furnish a cheap substitute for real virtue, permitting the spectator to satisfy himself with a simulacrum of morality at no inconvenience to himself or his vices.

We go to the theater to find a self-esteem which we do not deserve, to have a good opinion of ourselves, to share in the pride for great acts which we shall never commit, to be vain shadows of the great people we are shown. There we are prompt to embrace menaced virtue, to press it to our bosom. We are sure to triumph with it or we let go of it in time; we follow it to the foot of the scaffold but no farther, and no man put his head on the block next to the Count of Essex's [in Thomas Corneille's *Le Comte d'Essex*, 1678]. Thus we fill the pit but stay away from the places where suffering really takes place. If it were actually necessary to endure the fate of the unfortunates on the stage, the loges would be deserted. The poet, the painter, the sculptor, the actor are charlatans who sell us the firmness of old Horace and the patriotism of old Cato at little cost, in a word, the most seductive of flatterers. (*A.-T.*, XI, 143)

The gift of "sensitivity," the capacity to lend oneself to emotional experience, Diderot now saw as not just irrelevant to the issue of morality but perhaps antithetical to it. For if we satisfy our need for virtue, whether that need be instinctive or socially imposed, by a pleasurable gush of feeling, we are less, not more, disposed toward actually doing something good ourselves. Since we are all, at heart, a bit vicious, what distinguishes the good man from the bad is not how he feels, but what he does. Rejecting Shaftesbury's position that only motivation counts, Diderot imagined a new model of the virtuous man, one who spends his days performing actions which benefit humanity. Instead of going to the theater to weep over the plight of the unfortunate on the stage, he addresses himself to helping the unfortunate in reality. What sympathy he feels is probably better damped; it can only serve to distract him from his virtuous activities.

Diderot was becoming increasingly engrossed in his own "virtuous activities," spending a good part of his days helping people who turned up at his door with their problems. It was not the rather elegant commissions, such as conducting a young prince of Saxe-Gotha about Paris at Grimm's behest, which he especially enjoyed, but the humble ones, such as intervening in behalf of a poor servant girl, Louise Gedenère, whose clothes were being kept by her rascally brothers. Diderot loved to recount these stories, in which he played much the same role as his father used to play, to his family and friends. Particularly sweet were those occasions involving relatives from Langres whom the Abbé Didier had refused to aid. "Poor old Vigneron is dead, abandoned by his son-in-law and his own daughter," Diderot told his sister. "I had Monsieur the Abbé solicited to add one *écu* a month to what I was giving him. He has his reasons, good ones apparently, for succoring those outside his own family. I would laugh about it were it not for the atrocity of these principles" (*C.*, VIII, 50). There were other pleasurable moments, as when he wrote to David Hume (shortly after Rousseau, who had been Hume's guest, had quarreled with the Scottish philosopher) to request "if he were not totally disgusted with doing good," his assistance in finding a job for an unfortunate relative of Mme Diderot in London. "After all," said Diderot, "conversing with oneself while going to bed at night, one is more pleased with a good action than a beautiful page" (*C.*, VII, 221).

Some of his charities called upon the talent for "persiflage" he had demonstrated in duping M. de Croismare. A woman whom the Count de Saint-Florentin had seduced and abandoned turned to Diderot for help when she was destitute. Diderot wrote letters for her to her former lover, and they wrung a modest pension from him. In one such letter, for example, the discarded mistress was made to express herself as follows: "While I could live, Monseigneur, on the gifts of your tenderness, I never sought the aid of your pity; but all that I have left of your passion is your portrait. Tomorrow, if you do not remedy my poverty, I shall be obliged to sell it in order to have bread" (*C.*, VIII, 91).

Diderot was pleased with his position in the center of the spider's web. "It's a strange thing, the variety of my roles in this world. I cannot help laughing about it," he told Sophie. "They should call me Père Toutàtous!" (Father All-Things-to-All-Men). It was especially pleasant to remind his brother that one's actions were what counted in life, not one's thoughts.

Grimm, although frequently exploiting Diderot's willingness to engage himself in other people's affairs, had fallen into the habit of casting aspersions on the very generosity he was wont to abuse. King Stanislas, one of Grimm's favorite princes, wished to meet Diderot, but Grimm assured him that while "capable of disposing of his time and sharing with Voltaire the glory of genius, Diderot wastes it writing scraps, or uses it in a manner more afflicting still, abandoning it to all those who have the indiscretion to demand it" (*C.*, X, 91).

Being Father Toutàtous offered Diderot the great advantage of repudiating Shaftesbury's insistence on the primacy of intention, a position he had seen disastrously coopted by Rousseau. He began to ally himself instead with a new definition of the virtuous man: he who acted well even if he thought ill.

In his curious experimental dialogues—*Le Rêve de d'Alembert, L'Entretien de d'Alembert*, and the *Suite de l'entretien*, really one work in three parts, written in 1767 and circulated among a few friends—Diderot embodied this new conception of the man of virtue in the character of one Dr. Bordeu. The doctor, along with the butcher and the executioner, must subordinate his personal feelings to the demands of his technique. It is through the exercise of a skill, laboriously acquired and faithfully applied, that he succeeds in helping mankind, not by merging with the sufferer in a burst of empathy. The physician who "felt" with his patients might vomit when they did, and although this sensitivity might speak well for his capacity to empathize, it would in no way contribute to the well-being of the sick.

Diderot began *L'Entretien de d'Alembert* by a brutal frontal assault on the conception of the "ideal form of man," proposing that a statute by Huez (a mediocre sculptor) be smashed to bits, its materials mixed with humus, and consumed by a human being in the form of vegetables grown in the soil thus produced. In this way he resolved the problem of investing lifeless, idealized form with the vital functions in the most radical fashion. Not only did Diderot propose to destroy the statue in order, eventually, to eat it, an effective if drastic attempt at internalization, but he postulated that the material from which the statue had been made was endowed with potential sensibility from the beginning. Lacking only the organization necessary to produce the actions associated with sensibility, matter of any sort, from a pinch of dust to a human brain, shared a common essence.

Just as man differs from the rest of creation only by means of a distinctive organization, so his feelings and ideas, from the simplest to the most complex, are all only moments in the constant ebb and flow of his internal economy. After his conversation with Diderot, figuring in the dialogue as himself, d'Alembert goes to bed, and his Platonic friend Mlle de l'Espinasse reports his somnambulatory mutterings to Dr. Bordeu. D'Alembert's words and movements in his sleep reveal the permutations of the ideas they have been discussing; his utterances reflect the influence these ideas have on his body and reciprocally his physiological reactions shape the successive forms his ideas take.

"In this immense ocean of matter, no molecule like another, no molecule like itself for an instant: *Rerum novus nascitur ordo* is its eternal inscription." Then he added, sighing, "Oh vanity of our thoughts! Oh poverty of glory and our achievements! Oh misery! Oh smallness of our views! There is nothing solid but drinking, eating, loving, and sleeping. . . . Mlle de l'Espinasse, where are you?" "Here I am." Then his face got red. I tried to take his pulse but I did not know where he had hidden his hand. He seemed to undergo a convulsion. His mouth was half-opened, his breathing was rapid, he sighed deeply, and then softly, and then deeply again: he turned his head on his pillow and fell asleep. After a few minutes I saw a little smile wander over his lips, he said in a low voice: "On a planet where men multiplied like fish, where the sperm of a man pressed on the eggs of a woman . . . I would have fewer regrets." (*O.p.*, 301)

In imagining this scene between the scholarly d'Alembert and his friend—they both, incidentally, learned of the work's existence and were highly insulted by their roles in it—Diderot demonstrated his idea of the interaction between various parts of the human being, once sleep had stilled the voice of censorship. D'Alembert's thought flowed downward from the abstract to the organic, beginning with a theoretical statement about primal matter, to a paraphrase of Virgil, to a banal observation about the human condition containing the word "love," evoking a sexual reaction which in turn reminded him of Mlle de l'Espinasse. After he had satisfied his sexual desire, his postmasturbatory melancholy found expression in a fanciful speculation over the possibility of alternate means of generation. By reporting d'Alembert's thought processes while asleep, Diderot attempted to penetrate the opacity of the conscious personality, as in his eagerness to understand human physiology he read endless medical texts and badgered his doctor friends for precise anatomical information.[2]

Mlle de l'Espinasse, with her excessive sensitivity, and d'Alembert, with his arid *esprit de géométrie,* form an oddly complementary duo who could only approach a comprehension of reality by forcing their respective natures.[3] D'Alembert cannot permit his intuitive sensitivity to find expression except when sleep has dulled his conscious mind, whereas Julie de l'Espinasse requires the evenly applied pressure of Dr. Bordeu's logic to follow her own arguments without losing sight of their consequences in a rush of feeling. Bordeu effortlessly holds sway over the conversation; his self-awareness enables him, awake, to understand what d'Alembert can only murmur in his sleep, while his intellectual control lets him induce Julie de l'Espinasse to make explicit the truths which she but vaguely senses and would prefer to leave unformulated. No longer interested in exterior form as a guide to the personality,

Diderot had Bordeu describe himself from within, and the central aspect of his portrait is his continuing struggle to master his own sensitivity:

The great man, if he has unfortunately received this natural tendency [toward sensitivity], will constantly attempt to weaken it, to dominate it, to make himself the master of his movements and to leave all the powers in the brain (*l'origine du faisceau*). Then he will be self-possessed in the midst of great dangers, he will judge coldly, but sanely. Nothing that can serve his interests will escape him; it will be difficult to surprise him; he will be forty-five years old, he will be a great king, a great artist, above all a great actor, a great philosopher, great poet, great musician, great doctor; he will reign over himself and all he surveys. People with sensitivity, or fools, are on the stage, he is in the orchestra, he is the sage. (*O.p.,* 357)

Not quite prepared to present this description as a self-portrait Diderot applied it to a man on whom medical experience with the realities of life has conferred prestigious authority. As opposed to d'Alembert, whose monkish, abstract intellectualism is, in Diderot's eyes, an unsuccessful attempt to suppress the passions, culminating only in ridiculous sleep-befogged masturbation, Dr. Bordeu is able to taste pure pleasure and yet is always master of both his feelings and his thoughts.

In the character of Bordeu, Diderot negated Rousseau's twin ideals of emotivity and transparency.[4] As opposed to Rousseau's impulse to dissolve the self in a flood of feeling, Bordeu's goal was self-possession, implying both awareness and control. Against Rousseau's claims for the goodness of the inner self, enjoying its own diffuse sensations, Diderot pitted the non-sympathetic virtue of the technician. The physician exemplified Diderot's growing belief that sensitivity and positive action were antagonistic. Bordeu purchased his capacity to minister to the discomfort of his fellow human beings at the price of his feelings. In Diderot's view, the cumulative good effect of his acts not only compensated for, but was rendered possible by his separateness, his distance from others. D'Alembert, on the other hand, had not submerged himself in his emotions, but he had not mastered them either. Instead, he chose to ignore them. Like the "dear brother," Abbé Didier, whose denial of sexual realities Diderot tirelessly denounced, d'Alembert's mental life had restricted itself to a system of narrow formulae in which sensitivity was not dominated but suppressed.

Although Bordeu had earned the intellectual liberty to speculate daringly by his life of service to humanity, Diderot insisted that the doctor's morals were irreproachable. "Whatever judgment you form of my ideas," the doctor tells Julie de l'Espinasse in the *Suite de l'entretien,* after having elaborated for her benefit his notions of the utility of masturbation and the possibly interesting results of mating men with goats, "I hope, for my part, that you will not come to any conclusions against the honesty of my morals" (*O.p.,* 373). In a letter some years later, Diderot applied the same distinction to himself: "I beg you . . . not to judge me without having considered me, not to lose any extracts from this formless and dangerous production, publicity about which could destroy my repose, my fortune, my life, and my honor, or the just opinion people have conceived of my morals" (*C.,* IX, 157–158). However independent of the day's prejudices Diderot permitted himself to be in his mental life, he continued to feel the eyes of the public scrutinizing the philosopher's behavior. To d'Alembert in 1769 Diderot claimed that the dialogues had been destroyed at his request and only imperfectly reconstructed, referring to them as a "broken statue" (*C.,* IX, 157; *A.-T.,* IX, 251). The image is a persuasive one, for the "model philosopher," assembled from component parts "found in nature," had undergone a thorough vivisection and reintegration in the three dialogues. He continued to function as an integral element in Diderot's thinking, but he showed the marks of his experience.

In his celebrated analysis of the actor's art, the *Paradoxe sur le comédien,* Diderot discussed the role of the artist from the same point of view that he had assumed toward Dr. Bordeu in the three d'Alembert dialogues.[5] The self-awareness and self-control which he had attributed to his new version of the "ideal philosopher" now became the essential qualities of the actor: "I wish him to have great judgment; I want, in this man, a cold and tranquil spectator; I demand penetration and no sensitivity" (*O.e.,* 306). But it was not the actor alone who needed to stifle his sympathies; emotional control had become the *sine qua non* of artistic creation. "The great poets, the great actors, perhaps in general all the great imitators of nature, whoever they may be, gifted with a fine imagination, a great judgment, a fine tact, sure taste, are the least sensitive of beings. Sensitivity is scarcely the quality of a great genius. He will love justice, but he will exercise that virtue without experiencing its sweetness. It is not his heart, it is his head which does everything" (*O.e.,* 310).

Repudiating *in toto* the emotional merging he had counted as art's greatest quality in the *Eloge de Richardson,* Diderot now insisted upon the separation between the artist and the spectator, the artist carefully manipulating the spectator's feelings, wringing from him at will cries of pity or roars of laughter, while remaining completely untouched, not unlike Aristotle's godlike unmoved Mover. In this way the roles of the artist and the public were really reversed; it was the spectator who made a display of himself and the artist who observed in neutral silence. "In the great comedy, the comedy of the world, the one to which I always return, all the heated souls are on the stage; the men of genius are in the pit. The

former are called fools; the latter, who are busy depicting
their follies, are called sages" (O.e., 311).

Diderot had come at length to reject the aesthetic of sensitivity set forth earlier in the *Eloge de Richardson*. Whereas
in the *Eloge* he had extolled Richardson's ability to engage his
sympathies, to induce him to find pleasure in identifying with
suffering, he now regarded with contempt the role of the
spectator enjoying his own sensations of compassion. As an
artist he had detached himself from the public that had once
appeared so appealing and so menacing. Now he postulated
another metaphor for the relationship between the two. Rather
than constructing a "perfect model" of the artist for the spectator to glimpse behind the character, he suggested that the
actor's characterization be borne on the shoulders of the poet's
and "shut up in a great wicker mannequin of which it is the
soul."

He moves this mannequin in a terrifying way, even for the poet
who no longer recognizes himself in it, and he terrifies us just as
children frighten one another by holding their little doublets up
over their heads, and imitating to their best ability the raucous and
lugubrious voices of a phantom they are impersonating. Have
you never seen an urchin coming forward under the hideous mask
of an old crone hiding him from head to toe? Under this mask he
laughs at his little playmates fleeing in terror. This urchin is the
true symbol of the actor, his playmates are symbols of the spectator.
(O.e., 376)

Diderot's "statue," after being reduced to dust and consumed
in the *Entretien de d'Alembert*, had been transformed into a
great wicker mannequin, with the artist no longer outside,
mimicking perfection before the spectators, but inside, actively
manipulating them for his own purposes.

The pendulum of Diderot's thought had swung completely
to the side of technique. On one hand, the philosopher, or the

sage, as he liked to call himself,[6] was obliged to behave virtuously in all acts that were in any way public, in order both
to set a good example to the people and to avoid compromising his unorthodox ideas by giving rise to the suspicion that
they were merely justifications for a vicious temperament.
Diderot continued to take this function of his self-imposed
role very seriously. Telling Sophie how he had suffered during
an illness, he said, "Without the character of *philosophe,*
whose dignity must always be maintained, especially in the
eyes of the rabble surrounding us, I assure you that I would
have cried out more than once; instead, I had to sigh, bite
my lips, and writhe" (*C.,* III, 346). On the other hand, the
work of the sage—whether he be poet, artist, actor, novelist,
doctor, or statesman—was calculated to have a certain desired effect on the public. His "virtue" came to carry an
almost Aristotelian sense of proper functioning. As the "virtue"
of a knife is its ability to cut or the "virtue" of a doctor to cure,
the virtue of an actor is to make the spectator experience a
particular set of feelings.

At this point, however, Diderot's reasoning led him into an
impasse; between the skill of the technician manipulating man
to his own ends, and the imperative of the philosopher leading men to virtue, there would appear to be little common
ground, for the essence of virtue appeared more and more to
Diderot to be associated with self-awareness and self-control,
qualities that were not produced by manipulation. If the prin-
cipal asset of the "imitators of nature," as Diderot termed
artists, poets, etc., was the ability to dupe, to produce an illusion, how could this capacity ever be used to promote lucidity?

Before Diderot attempted to resolve this problem in *Jacques
le fataliste* he became involved in a series of events that modified his perceptions of the philosopher's role. In the course of
the project of self-examination which he had undertaken with

Sophie, he experienced a withdrawal from his friends and, at the same time, an awakened interest in his daughter, Angélique, who in 1762 was nine years old. He began to take a more active part in her education. Having for many years only bemoaned her fate under the tutelage of her bigoted mother, he now began to spend some of the hours with her which he had formerly spent with his friends. "I had my little one practice her piano lesson," he told Sophie. "This is a task I have imposed upon myself because I like it and it is useful to her; one which I scarcely ever fail to perform" (*C.*, IV, 109). He attempted to combat Mme Diderot's influence by teaching the girl what he felt was vital to her intellectual growth. He became increasingly engrossed in her; fatherhood had become not merely a theoretical subject calling forth idealistic effusions, but a practical activity.

Diderot found an extra advantage in working on Angélique's upbringing: it permitted him to denounce his pious brother in better conscience. Didier's celibacy marked him as a moral imbecile: "You must either be wicked or mad because you live alone," Diderot told him, using the same words which had once infuriated Rousseau, but with the confidence of one who no longer has any reproach to fear. Having rejected the idea that virtue was somehow an essential quality, he increasingly emphasized the importance of actions. In a burst of enthusiasm for his role of exemplary father, he offered to sell his library, the very heart of his intellectual life, in order to provide Angélique with a fine dowry. Since she was only nine years old at the time, the issue could hardly have been pressing, and one senses a certain taste for melodrama in Diderot's insistence that "the philosopher let himself be despoiled by the husband and father" (*C.*, V, 28). Fortunately for the philosopher, Catherine of Russia got wind of the offer and purchased the library with the stipulation that he enjoy its use during his lifetime. The whole affair flattered Diderot immensely. As Catherine had undoubtedly calculated, her purchase had procured for her not only a library but an important friend in the West.

Diderot began to discover that Angélique, unlike his family and many of his friends, amply repaid the attention he invested in her. He convinced himself that she possessed a superior mind and was capable of great intellectual achievement. He delighted in discovering echoes of his own thought in her remarks, and particularly appreciated Angélique's grasp of the distinction between piety and morality. "I am crazy about my daughter," he told Sophie. "She says that her mother prays to God and that her father does good deeds" (*C.*, VIII, 231).

He explained in detail to Angélique the differences between the sexes, even had her attend anatomy classes (much to the horror of Didier) so that she could satisfy her curiosity and be protected from the possibly dangerous effects of things being left to her imagination. He was enchanted with her common sense, her reasonable replies to his questions. And yet, as she approached marriageable age, he felt increasingly uneasy.

The question of Angélique's future reopened the whole issue of his own identity, and while getting her settled down he was obliged to reconsider compromises decided upon years before. He had tried to educate Angélique to be free from prejudices, liberated from the superstitions and conventions of a corrupt society. She was not merely the daughter, but in some ways the disciple of a philosopher. There were young women of Diderot's acquaintance, although not many, who were leading independent lives, who had made careers for themselves, and married later rather than sooner. Indeed, some had not married at all. But Mlle de Bihiran, who held the anatomy classes which Angélique attended, or Mlle Collet, the sculptor and protégée of Diderot's friend Falconet, or Mlle Jodin, an actress to whose personal and financial affairs he devoted many patient hours, seemed to exist under a kind of shadow; their marginal status troubled Diderot. In his letters to Falconet he never tired of admonishing him to marry Mlle Collet, and he repeatedly, although it appears fruitlessly, warned Mlle Jodin against the seductions of unprincipled men.

For Diderot as philosopher, the sexual act itself was one "for which men were to be congratulated and women scarcely to be blamed," a mere "voluptuous rubbing of two intestines" (C., IV, 120). Yet in his role as father, along with the anatomy lessons, he gave stern warnings against the social disasters incurred by the woman who lets herself be seduced. Here is how he interpreted the tender words of a suitor to Angélique: "What does 'I love you' mean? It signifies, Mademoiselle, that if you would be so kind as to dishonor yourself, lose your status in life, be banished from society, lock yourself up forever in a convent, and cause your mother and father to die of shame, all for my sake, I would really be obliged" (C., VIII, 231).

In spite of her fine mind and her liberated spirit, Angélique was to obey the most conventional of society's dicta regarding the behavior of women; to be exact, the society of Langres, whose critical gaze Diderot still felt on the back of his neck. It was impossible to let Angélique lead her own life as a professional musician because part of her was held in ransom to Diderot's family. He had not lost his need to prove to them that the philosophic way of life led to virtue, and the only virtue they recognized was defined by the proprieties of bourgeois provincial life. Diderot was torn between his desire to astonish his family with his daughter's perfect conventionality and his impulse to turn her into a female *philosophe*.

"There is a little *Treatise on Human Nature* [Hobbes] which I would have used as my daughter's catechism, if one were free to raise a child according to one's fantasy" (C., XII, 46, note

6), he told Sophie, and in another letter, "What a journey I could make that mind embark upon if I dared! It would only be a matter of leaving a few books lying about" (*C.*, VIII, 232). But he did not dare, and Angélique matured a divided creature, confusedly trying to please her father by behaving like a convent girl and thinking like a middle-aged philosopher.

A curious expedient suggested itself to Diderot, one which, bizarre as it seemed, might well have resolved the issue satisfactorily. He would marry her to Grimm. Although Grimm was, to be sure, forty-five years old and long the lover of another woman, Angélique could turn such deficits to good advantage. As his wife, she could lead an intellectual life among the *philosophes,* free to make the same discreet sentimental arrangements as they.

Diderot's letters to Grimm, coquettishly enumerating the charms of his sixteen-year-old daughter, have a pathetic ring: "It would be a great pleasure for her if you heard her play some pieces [on the harpsichord]. I believe she plays well, but what I am almost sure of is that she will be a musician, that she will know the theory of the art, unless a son-in-law comes along and ruins it all, spoiling the little person's figure and taking away her taste for study. I kiss you for her although she would do it much better than I and give you more pleasure" (*C.*, IX, 189–90).

Not long after he was taking a more positive father-in-lawish tone: "If you marry her you will have, I swear, a pretty wife, but one with whom I would advise you to walk a straight path" (*C.*, IX, 200). But whether it was the straight path that put him off or Grimm's natural aversion to women without titles or fortunes, or some other reason, Diderot quickly sensed his friend's lack of interest and dropped the subject—although not cavalierly, for Grimm, it should be remembered, was "the other half of himself," his "dear hermaphrodite" (*A.-T.*, XVIII, 238).

After a few more tentative essays in the intellectual milieu, such as Diderot's remark to Sedaine: "Ah, my dear friend, were you not so old I would give you my daughter!" and some vague negotiations with Vialet, an acquaintance of Sophie Volland, he settled upon a young man from Langres, Caroillon de Vandeul. Angélique herself, perhaps mortified by the unsuccessful attempts at marrying her into the "*philosophes*' boutique," appeared to be delighted with her fiancé. No sooner had the marriage been agreed upon, however, than Diderot began to regret it; Vandeul was too interested in the financial side of the wedding and too little in the romantic. Vandeul was driving a hard bargain, showing none of the heedless passion which Diderot imagined in a son-in-law: "He is managing to go to bed cheap with a pretty woman, both rich and well brought up, and running the risk of some day inheriting a hundred thousand *écus*, without putting in much himself," he grumbled to Grimm. "I am indifferent to money and uncalculating. My son-in-law should resemble me" (*C.*, XI, 141–42). Preparations for the marriage irritated him; time and time again he was on the verge of dismissing Vandeul and reclaiming Angélique. But, distasteful as the protracted negotiations became, they presented one redeeming feature of considerable importance to Diderot: they allowed him to return to Langres and be publicly admired at his brother's expense.

The appetite of *tout Langres* was whetted by the spicy affair. Would the intransigent Abbé finally now, in 1772, after more than twenty years, put his seal to Diderot's life by officiating at Angélique's wedding? Vandeul's family was the very model of the prosperous provincial bourgeoisie, and the marriage placed Diderot squarely in the ranks of proper fathers. The Abbé held firm, however, resisting all blandishments, even a letter from Angélique (too pathetic not to have been dictated by her father), begging him to preside at the ceremony: "Do you believe that a well-bred niece would not rather receive the benediction of her uncle than that of the greatest bishop in the world? There is, however, one such bishop and not the least respected either, who himself offered me this honor; but it is by you that I would wish to have my hand placed in Caroillon's" (C., XII, 106–107). The crusty old country priest was not at all moved by this appeal to family sentiment. "You are not and you never will be my niece," he informed her, "and you and M. Caroillon will be forbidden to enter my home, as is your father, for the same reason—religion" (C., XII, 113).

The Abbé had clearly put himself in a bad light. Old friends and neighbors from Langres attempted to intercede, but, as Diderot triumphantly explained to Grimm, "with each effort they make the 'saint' look uglier and the philosopher more beautiful" (C., X, 126). Finally all of Langres agreed, or so Diderot believed, that the impious black sheep had revealed himself as the true son of the father while the priest turned out to be a despicable bigot. "If my father returned to earth and [our sister] told him the story of your behavior and mine, the priest would leave charged with his malediction, as he is charged with the opprobrium of those who know the situation, and he would not refuse his blessing to his child, the *philosophe*" (C., XII, 161–62).

The Abbé's obstinacy finally freed Diderot from the constraint he had been living under for so many years. All efforts at appeasement had been fruitless; Didier would unquestionably disinherit his niece, and there was nothing more to be gained by attempting to change his mind. The promise made twelve years earlier, not to publish anything against religion, had failed, after all, to sway the Abbé. Diderot, at the same time proud of his well-played role in settling his daughter and angry at the world—at Vandeul for being greedy, at his wife for being unpleasant, at Angélique for being married—

took the occasion to tell his brother off definitively and to withdraw his promise.

Diderot found himself miserably alone after Angélique's marriage. "Mme Diderot and I prowl about one another, but we are no longer anything to each other" (*C.*, XII, 140). Nor could he find much solace in visiting the young couple, because his son-in-law was "half pompous, half conceited," and seemed to Diderot bent on turning his bride into an animated doll. "He finds that she does not have enough dresses. It would take dresses, I believe, for all the hours of the day to satisfy the vanity of my little florist, who would like, for his pastime, to see his poor little tulip bloom in a different way every minute" (*C.*, XII, 178–79).

His misery was somewhat relieved, however, by the realization that he was suffering not only from loneliness but from seeing Angélique the wife of another man. "Who would believe that a sensible father could experience such silly jealousy? This discovery, which made me laugh, soothed me a great deal" (*C.*, XII, 146). At length he relinquished the ungrateful role of disapproving father he was playing in Angélique's life and made up his mind to embark on the long-deferred voyage to Russia, in order to express his gratitude to Catherine personally.

5/Adviser to the Empress

For Diderot each calling in life was associated with a technical virtue. It was the function of the magistrate to distribute justice in accordance with the laws, that of the artist to imitate nature, that of the sovereign to promote the well-being of his subjects. The philosopher's role was also based on an activity: he was to instruct the magistrate in the meaning of justice, the artist in an understanding of nature, and the sovereign in the basis of the people's well-being. In this way, philosophy was envisaged not only as a useful activity but as the pivotal guide to virtue for a whole society. The virtue of the philosopher himself, however, remained technical; it depended on how well or how ill he fulfilled his educative function. If the magistrate dispensed justice badly, after having been enlightened by the philosopher, it was he who was at fault, not the philosopher himself.

Catherine's invitation to visit Russia presented Diderot with the opportunity to function as a philosopher on the highest level. He would advise her as to the proper legislation to be introduced in the country in order to bring its laws into accordance with those of nature. Were she to accept his suggestions, all the better; but the most important aspect of the voyage for Diderot was the realization of his own program. Diderot has frequently been called naïve in his relations with the despotic Empress of Russia.[1] It should be borne in mind, however, that although he always spoke of her in the most flattering terms, frequently describing her as combining "the soul of Brutus with the face of Cleopatra" (C., XIV, 13), he was obliged to demonstrate gratitude toward her for purchasing his library, and that any criticism of her in a letter could have been the occasion for what Diderot most detested, a public scandal compromising the behavior of a *philosophe*. Was Catherine secretly mocking the earnest, bourgeois Frenchman who thumped her on the knee as he outlined his plans for bringing justice and reason to bear on the structures of Russian society? Was she so bored with the half-savage aristocrats of her snowbound capital that she tolerated Diderot's preaching for the sake of his company? It is not possible to answer these questions with certitude, for if ever a human being was born knowing the principles of the *Paradoxe sur le comédien* by heart, it was she. The woman who had seized the throne of Russia by arranging for her husband, Peter III, to be assassinated by her lover, knew how to keep her thoughts to herself.

But for Diderot it mattered less that a given program be instituted in Russia than that it be proposed by a philosopher. To the extent that he was disappointed by his experiences with Catherine, he seemed disgruntled that a limited creature like her should have been given the opportunity to rule Russia instead of himself. He left her with a curious manuscript, in the words of Maurice Tourneux, "a series of chapters which, lacking any particular link between them, were to provoke the meditations of his interlocutor after their separation." Near the end of these astonishingly frank pages, Diderot confided, "I may have been indiscreet, or thoughtless, but I have here, on the left side, a severe censor who tells me I was neither false nor wicked." He offered Catherine his best thinking on a variety of problems in Russian society, from the proper method of dealing with education to the desirability of introducing bathing among her subjects. He referred to himself, only half jokingly, as King Denis, and painted a description of his reign by which Catherine might judge her own. "If a sovereign had tried the happiness of a good sovereign," he told her, "he would never be able to renounce it. A father who isolates himself from his children, a king who isolates himself from his subjects, these are two monstrous beings to me." But he did not seem to entertain any serious expectations that she would adopt his ideas, nor was it his business as a philosopher to do so. "The philosopher awaits the fiftieth good king who will profit from his labors. While waiting he enlightens men upon their inalienable rights." [2]

The favor Diderot enjoyed at Catherine's court ignited sparks of jealousy from Saint Petersburg to Paris and back again by way of Ferney and Potsdam. As Diderot remarked, "the absent are always wrong," and had he been of a mind to feel persecuted, the malicious gossip spread about him would have amply justified paranoia. "What do you think of our philosopher?" asked one of Diderot's "friends," the Abbé Galiani, in a letter from Naples to Antoine-Léonard Thomas. "They are spreading terrible things about his conduct with the Tsarina. They say he dared to throw his wig in her face, pinch her knee, etc. He is unique, this Diderot, his head is the storehouse of the world; he knows everything and sometimes appears to know nothing. I believe he has as many mental lapses as most of the great men of Bicêtre [a madhouse near Paris]" (C., XIII, 134). Frederick of Prussia was especially infuriated by Diderot's success, fearing, quite rightly, that he would attempt to discredit the Potsdam alliance in Catherine's eyes. Diderot never failed to denigrate the King of Prussia before Catherine, often in a rather earthy way, suggesting, for example, that "if one knew where they incubated the Fredericks, a good man would go break all the eggs and work on hatching the Catherines" (*C.*, XIII, 200).

Diderot was well aware that his enemies and his "friends" were watching his movements with the eager curiosity of malice. The accusation, however, to which he felt vulnerable was not the one of naïveté or eccentricity but of calculation. Catherine's apologist in the West could have reasonably expected a fortune; Diderot was in a position to see the end of his financial worries for life. In 1767 Rousseau had faced a similar dilemma when King George III had offered him a pension at the suggestion of David Hume. He first reacted by refusing it in a gesture of independence, as he had refused the pensions of Louis XV and Frederick of Prussia; then, tempted to accept it if hedged by all sorts of conditions that would nullify the significance of acceptance, he finally turned on Hume and his friends who were conducting the negotiations, and accused them of trying to make him betray himself.[3]

Diderot, sensing the dangers of a debacle of his own based on a similar mixture of feelings, devised an adroit strategy to protect himself. He drew up an elaborate "Peace Treaty between a great Sovereign and a *philosophe*," in which he stipulated that Catherine grant him three favors: his expenses during the voyage back to Paris, an officer to accompany him safely home, and lastly, a memento of her Imperial Majesty, a "bagatelle" valuable only because she had used it. Beyond this Diderot would accept nothing because, as he wrote to Sophie, "I did not want the Russians to say that, on the pretext of coming to thank her for her former favors, I had solicited new ones; the French, that [when he praised Catherine] instead of the truth they were hearing the questionable voice of gratitude" (*C.*, XIII, 208). Or, as he put it more succinctly to his wife: "I said to myself, 'I must shut the mouth of that rabble' " (*C.*, XIII, 232). Before leaving Russia Diderot made it his business that the story of Catherine's generosity and his own firmness be as widely circulated as possible. The voyage to Russia and his discussions with Catherine were constructed as a kind of theater, Diderot at once writing the scenario and enacting the *beau rôle*. The last act would show the poor but proud *philosophe* enthusiastically describing the Tsarina to Paris at large in the most flattering way.

But theater was in no way to be confused with real life, and in his private calculations he was willing to profit from Catherine's largesse if he could so do without compromising the public image of the philosopher. To his wife he wrote: "I cannot believe that is all we have to expect from a sovereign who is generosity itself, for whom at an advanced age I did more than fifteen hundred leagues, and for whom I labored in every possible way, almost night and day for five months. Also my guide [a Greek, M. Bala] insinuated the opposite" (*C.*, XIII, 230).

Diderot's *philosophe* was his own creation, giving performances finely calculated to impress the audience. His self-esteem was more and more founded on pride in his mastery of the manipulation, not upon public opinion, "that malicious beast" (*O.r.*, 834).

Six of Diderot's most interesting works were produced during the brief and tumultuous period between Angélique's engagement and his return from Russia. It is difficult to ascribe exact dates to the *Entretien d'un père avec ses enfants, Ceci n'est pas un conte, Sur l'inconséquence du jugement publique, Le Supplément au voyage de Bougainville, L'Entretien d'un philosophe avec la Maréchale de xxx,* and *Jacques le fataliste,* but all appear to have been written between 1771 and 1774, and are so closely related in form and direction that they can be considered as a kind of unit in which Diderot re-examined once more his thinking on the problems of how to be virtuous in relation to nature and society.[4]

In these tales, the man who had advised an Empress, established a daughter, and told off a priest addressed the problem of virtue as an equal. Leaving aside for the moment *Jacques le fataliste*, the five tales present, in dialogue form, the situation of the individual man who must examine the guidelines put forth for human conduct and evaluate their relevance to him. Whereas, in his relations with Catherine, Diderot had been obliged to consider morality from the point of view of the legislator, in these works the questions are discussed exclusively in relation to the individual member of society.

The Catholic Church continued to direct the consciences of the faithful while the laws regulated the conduct of the citizens. Beyond these two bastions of traditional authority lay the whole intermediary zone of the proprieties, the unofficial rule of iron based upon usage, convention, and "what people will say." But above these local laws, particular religious beliefs, and specifically French social customs there existed a larger cultural tradition to which one might turn for guidance: the corpus of human standards summarized as European civilization. Western society, taken as an abstraction and divested of its purely accidental and local elements, could be viewed as a reliable index of man's best moral thought. In the five tales Diderot examined the claims of these authoritative guides by the criteria of reason and experience.

The works all shared essentially the same form: an anecdote or a series of memories was the occasion for comments from various characters who interpreted events from their personal viewpoints. Each dialogue had as its center an almost concrete chunk of reality, which was the subject of the complex discussions surrounding it. Diderot presented himself in the conversations as the *philosophe*, a man on whom many years of struggle with the problems of morality and many years of service to his fellow men had conferred an unshakable authority.

The materials and the plan of the *Entretien d'un père avec ses enfants* are virtually the same as for the other pieces: stories are recounted and interrupted, eliciting comments from the personae of the drama, who are the members of Diderot's own family and some of their friends and neighbors. The form is essentially open-ended, prohibiting by its very structure any real closure in the reader's mind such as would occur if the issues raised were definitely resolved. In fact, as we know from Paul Vernière's careful establishment of the varying texts, Diderot returned to the manuscript repeatedly, adding new anecdotes which served to render the presentation of the central problem more nuanced. But the problem itself may be stated easily: does not the law of the land represent an embodiment of the principle of justice which all good men are conscience-bound to obey? May we not consider ourselves just if we follow the law?

The affective center of the dialogue is Diderot's father. He is seated by the fire with his children—the Abbé Didier, the *philosophe,* and their sister. A series of secondary personages enter and leave the scene, Dr. Bissei, a prior, a notary, a hatter, and a retired engineer. Diderot's father recounts the story of how he once found himself in a difficult moral predicament. He had been asked to inventory the effects of a deceased priest. As he was sorting the papers, the priest's relatives, a poverty-stricken lot of wretched peasants, crowded around the door, waiting to receive their portion of the estate. As Diderot *père* was examining the documents he came across a will disinheriting the miserable relatives and leaving everything to a rich publisher in Paris. To have burned the patently inhumane will would have been the work of a moment; yet legally there was no question that the publisher was the rightful heir.

This story is interrupted by another. Dr. Bissei arrives, announcing that he has just come from the bedside of a notorious scoundrel whose life he intends to save if possible. Then the hatter presents *his* problem to Diderot's father: he spent his last twenty thousand louis d'or caring for his wife during her terminal illness. After her death he appropriated twenty thousand louis that were legally to go to a distant relative. He felt morally entitled to the money but his conscience reproached him. And the last anecdote is offered by Abbé Didier, taken from a description of life in Sicily. A virtuous Sicilian finds life intolerable in a country where the laws are flaunted daily. He takes it upon himself to be the judge, jury, and executioner of all criminals in Messina. Having dispatched more than fifty miscreants he presents himself before the viceroy, saying: "I have done your duty" (*O.p.*, 440). What should the viceroy do?

In the discussion of these examples of justice and the law, the Abbé Didier invariably favors following the legally prescribed conduct to the letter. The law is to be obeyed regardless of circumstances or consequences. Diderot treated his brother fairly in this dialogue, presenting his position as both rational and consistent, if devoid of compassion. The father, although he follows the law also, does so only after considerable hesitation, weighing the human factors. And the sister seems to be convinced by whichever argument she heard last.

Diderot himself, in each instance, judges the law by the twin standards of justice and benefaction. Natural man was anterior to legal man, and Diderot did not feel that he was assured of doing the right thing if his conscience contradicted the dicta of the law. "Is not the reason of the human race more sacred than the reason of the legislator?" he asks his father, who answers him gently: "My son, reason is a good pillow, but I find that my head rests more sweetly on that of religion and law" (*O.p.*, 436).

But Diderot's father is religious, his desire to be virtuous does not have the same roots as his son's. For Diderot the quest is not for a "good pillow," but rather for a coherent system of values that meets the test of his conscience. In Diderot's view his father should have consigned the unjust will to the flames, taking upon himself whatever consequences might have resulted from the action. His father, however, preferred to turn the question over to a moral authority, Father Bouin, who firmly recommended that the will be preserved. Diderot calls his father a "man of excellent judgment, but pious," as though that attribute had come to represent to him an unfortunate limitation. As for Dr. Bissei, Diderot stoutly maintains that he should have dispatched his criminal patient on the spot, his duty as a man outweighing his ethics as a doctor. The technical virtue of the physician needs to be administered by the higher virtue of the good man. While his partners in the dialogue try to define what every good man should do in the various circumstances, Diderot insists upon what *he* would have done. His approach to the moral issues raised is deliberately personal, it is his own ethics he wished to clarify, and all those who feel sufficiently worthy are invited to do likewise. "Nature made good laws for all eternity; the force which assures their execution is legitimate; and this force, which can do everything against the wicked man can do nothing against the good man. I am that good man and in these circumstances as in many others I summon it before the tribunal of my heart, of my reason, of my conscience, before the tribunal of natural equity. I interrogate it, submit to it, or declare it null and void" (*O.p.*, 430).

Diderot puts forth the most radically individualistic program possible for social man in this tale. It is not the laws which would judge him but he who would judge the laws. His father repeatedly raises the obvious objection of general applicability: "Preach these principles from the rooftops, I promise they will make your fortune and you will see the beautiful results." Diderot is very firm; these are not rules for the masses: "I shall not preach them; there are truths which are not made for fools;

but I will keep them for myself. 'For you who are a sage?' 'Certainly.'" At the end of the work, he shows his father in effect approving this exceptional view of himself. As Diderot kisses him good-night, he whispers: "'My Father, strictly speaking, there are no rules for the sage. . . .' 'Speak more softly,'" said his father. "'Since they are all subject to exceptions, it is up to him to judge the cases where one must submit to them or disregard them.' 'I wouldn't mind too much,'" replied the father, "'if, in a city, there were one or two citizens like you, but if they all thought the same, I would not live there'" (*O.p.,* 443).

Ceci n'est pas un conte, Le Supplément au voyage de Bougainville, and *Sur l'inconséquence du jugement publique* all appear to have been written within a few weeks of Angélique's wedding, and form a critique of Diderot's attitudes toward morality in sexual relations. Diderot, or his persona in *Sur l'inconséquence* . . . , recounts an anecdote of Mme de la Carlière, who, aware of the fleeting nature of passion and the hollowness of the marriage vows, attempted to found her union with Desroches on a more rational basis. Believing that he would not be constrained to fidelity by his promises before God, she induced him to swear before a group of their social equals. The question which Diderot raises is whether social pressures such as the threat of ostracism from the group can be substituted for the discounted punishments of religion. Desroches was eventually unfaithful to his wife anyway, because the way people live is invariably closer to nature than society's idealized picture of itself. The vows of eternal faithfulness are the debt paid to man's dream of virtue; the clandestine affairs are what is owed to nature. Desroches swore and Desroches strayed; to this extent the characters enacted the scenario decreed by a divided society. It was in keeping with custom for the amorous bridegroom to promise constancy; it was equally traditional for the husband of some years to seek adventure outside of marriage. But Desroches had made the other vow, the one that was not conventional, before the guests assembled at his wedding, and it was the consequences of this promise which interested Diderot. Mme de la Carlière, who had been convinced that shame before his social equals would have been infinitely harder for Desroches to bear than fear of divine retribution, reassembled the wedding guests and publicly denounced him.

The "little law" of conventions, usages, and formulas, although perhaps even more generally obeyed than the great law inscribed in the statute books, could not be bent by one person alone to serve a moral purpose. Mme de la Carlière was pitied and then blamed, Desroches damned and exculpated by an essentially frivolous and corrupt society which, at bottom, found the whole affair somewhat ridiculous. Diderot expresses his assessment of the value of public opinion in moral matters: "Here I ask you to turn your eyes from Mme de la Carlière and fix them on the public, on that imbecile crowd which judges us, which disposes of our honor, which lifts us to the clouds or drags us in the mud" (*O.r.*, 829).

The "imbecile crowd" vacillated in its judgment but ultimately, because of circumstances having nothing to do with Desroches's infidelity, it pronounced him guilty. Diderot declares, at the end of the tale, that if he had a daughter to marry he would not hesitate to give her to Desroches, based on his own judgment of his character. For, says Diderot, his conduct was irreproachable except for his one mistake, and as for that, "I have my ideas, perhaps just, certainly bizarre, about certain actions, which I regard less as the vices of men than as the consequences of our absurd legislation, source of mores equally absurd and of a depravity I would term artificial. That is not very clear but it will clarify itself perhaps another time" (*O.r.*, 835). Both the official law of the land and the unofficial law of public opinion had been weighed in the scale and found wanting. Diderot dismisses his contemporaries as "impertinent gossips whose approval or disapproval are worth nothing in the conduct of one's life" (*O.r.*, 815).

These two pieces, largely destructive in tone, conveyed the philosopher's sense of autonomy, at once proud of himself and contemptuous toward others. But the problem of establishing a rational code of morality in harmony with nature, one whereby the individual would not be sacrificed to arbitrary laws and hypocritical customs, remained largely unresolved. After his daughter's wedding Diderot composed another piece, *Le Supplément au voyage de Bougainville*, in which he clarified his ideas about "certain actions."

Nothing could reveal the diversity of temperament between Rousseau and Diderot more sharply than their respective attempts to reconcile sexuality and morality in a primitive paradise. Rousseau had received his first two discourses like a vision. "Let us put aside the facts," [5] he asked the reader; the reality he was about to describe sprang from the uncontaminated sources of his own being. Civilization, with its burdensome conventions and insistence on contractual obligations, had placed an intolerable restraint on man's sexuality. Rousseau dreamed of a world in which arousal and satisfaction were all but simultaneous, where the woman coveted was the woman possessed, and no artificial delay intervened letting secondary complications gain purchase. The great obstacle to such a program was, of course, the child. The act which Rousseau felt should have been delightfully void of consequence was, on the contrary, the commencement of an enmeshing web of obligations. Rousseau's solution was to imagine even the family as an unnatural perversion, invented by society to stifle man's spontaneity. In nature man and woman would couple wordlessly, fortuitously, parting as soon as their need has been satisfied.[6] When the woman, as self-absorbed as the man, bore her child, she would carry it about on her body as an undifferentiated appendage until it was able to walk, at which point it would wander off to assume its own solitary existence. None of the three would even recognize each other were they to meet again. Only in this way would man be really free sexually. Even the libertine in Europe was hampered by the obligation to seduce, involving him in complex rituals compared to the immediate gratification of which Rousseau dreamed.

Diderot's paradise, although as much a portrait of its author's soul as Rousseau's, was derived from the very reputable account of the first French voyage to Tahiti by Louis-Antoine de Bougainville (1766–69). The elements drawn from Bougainville were reworked and reshaped by Diderot until their original contours all but disappeared. Nevertheless, the irreducible core of material drawn from reality was as central to the *Supplément* as to Diderot's other tales; it anchored his imagination in the world.

Where Rousseau resolved the conflict with moral duty by denying that the child in nature even needed a family, Diderot imagined instead a whole society whose very reason for being was the child. His Tahitians did not accumulate lifeless gold, like the denatured Europeans; they collected children and calculated an individual's wealth by the number of babes asleep under his roof. "The entire island offered the image of a single large family, and each hut was like the different rooms of one of our large houses" (*O.p.*, 504). Conception, far from being the inconvenience or even calamity associated with intercourse that it was in European countries, represented the blessing of nature to the Tahitians. The nubile girl was divested of the chaste garment she had worn as a child and was permitted to bestow her favors on whomever she wished. When she chose to leave her lover's hut for that of another, her children came with her as a highly desirable dowry. Artificial barriers between the sexes, such as those imposed in

Europe, did not exist. Even incest was accepted, especially where a benevolent father was attempting to help an unattractive daughter by providing her with children. In civilized France, Diderot had felt driven to the point of selling his library to amass a dowry for his daughter; how infinitely more agreeable were the duties of fatherhood in Tahiti!

In place of Rousseau's dream of the isolated individual, at once subject to and nurtured by nature alone, Diderot envisioned a society that would resemble the living organism he described in *Le Rêve de d'Alembert*. Each person should be a functioning part of the larger network of reciprocal bonds. The good society, like the healthy plant, would demonstrate its vigor by its fertility, and the Tahitians believed they had gotten the best of the bargain by permitting their women to sleep with the French: "You show us a gratitude that makes us laugh," says Orou, the spokesman for the natives. "We thank you, for we have placed upon you and your companions the strongest of all impositions. Our wives and daughters have come to draw the blood from your veins" (*O.p.,* 500).

For Diderot the central virtue of Tahitian culture was not that it was liberated from law, that primitive anarchy would be preferable to civilized order, but that the islanders' laws, customs, and religion were based upon nature and in harmony with her designs. Unlike the European who was constantly torn between the demands of contradictory authorities, the Tahitian was permitted to experience himself as a whole. The voice of nature and the voice of society were in unison and the word they spoke was: procreate.

A society based on procreation. For Diderot, simple sexual pleasure was all very well, but the real erotic paradise was populated with pregnant women. "As for me, that condition has always been moving," he told Sophie (*C.,* IV, 83), "a pregnant woman interests me." Activity should be productive, sexuality was a kind of pleasant work which ideally turned out practical results. This was the main reason Diderot favored legalizing divorce. The woman, like the earth, could only be said to belong to a man as long as he actively used her for the purpose which nature intended. Absentee landlordship, or the right of ownership without use, was an abuse of the fertility of both. "The tyranny of man has converted the possession of woman into property," he remarked disapprovingly.[7]

At the end of the *Supplément*, the partners in the dialogue, agreeing that European laws violated those of nature and did not contribute to man's happiness, address themselves to the problem of action. What should the sage do in a corrupt and self-contradictory society? " 'What will we do? Will we go back to nature? Will we submit ourselves to the laws?' "

" 'We will speak out against senseless laws until they are reformed, and in waiting, we will submit to them.' " It was a two-part program; the sage must demonstrate exemplary firmness by publicly respecting the laws and usages of his country, because "he who, of his own private authority, violates a bad law, authorizes everyone else to violate a good one" (*O.p.*, 515). But this consideration regulated only his public actions, not his conscience, for as Diderot had insisted in the *Entretien d'un père avec ses enfants*, the sage was capable of deciding which problems could be disposed of in private without ever coming to public attention. Thus Diderot would have burned the priest's unjust will without hesitation, but he would have done so secretly, not because he felt guilty but to avoid setting a bad example before the common people.

Obeying the law, however, was not the same thing as believing it just, and if the sage were bound to obey by his respect for order, he was equally obliged to work for the reform of the existing system. The true philosopher did not hide in the forest to escape the ravages of civilization, nor did he hatch violent plots to overthrow it. His duty was to realize its own ideals in his public role and to use the prestige he gained in so doing in order to ameliorate it. Like the actor in the *Paradoxe sur le comédien*, the philosopher's behavior before the world was contrived to produce a desired effect and need have no connection with his inner convictions.

During his stay in Holland on the way back to Paris from Russia, Diderot composed another dialogue, *L'Entretien d'un philosophe avec la Maréchale de xxx*, in which his creation, the philosopher, discusses the role of religion as a guide to virtue. His interlocutor is no longer some scruffy nephew of Rameau, nor a modest initial (as in the *Supplément*), but a Maréchale of France who receives him at her *toilette*. The intimate of Catherine the Great is not to be flustered by such an interview; the subject is morality and Diderot treats the participants in his dialogue as moral equals. The Maréchale obeys the precepts of her religion as part of a commerce with God. If she were not afraid of eternal damnation, in her words, "If I had nothing to hope or to fear when I am gone, there are many little pleasures of which I would not deprive myself" (*O.p.*, 527). But Diderot is not at all interested in the ethical value of her religious belief; whether she obeys the Church's commandments because she loves God or because she fears Him is not important. It is rather the efficacy of religious persuasion to improve conduct that he is investigating, subjecting Bayle's old contention—that a society of atheists would be no worse than a society of Christians—to the test of the individual believer. The philosopher and the Maréchale quickly agree that principles, whether those of the atheist or those of the devout, do not influence conduct to any marked degree.

"How can you be an honest man when bad principles join the passions to lead you toward evil?"

"I am inconsistent. Is there anything more common than being inconsistent?"

"Alas! Unfortunately not: people believe and every day behave as if they did not."

"And without believing, one conducts oneself more or less as if one believed." (*O.r.*, 529)

Rousseau's painful charge, that it was impossible to be virtuous without religion, is refuted in this dialogue, not by means of angry polemic but by the most amicable and urbane tête-à-tête. As Diderot was fond of telling his brother, even Archbishops discussed religion with him calmly, acknowledging that "the atheist may nevertheless be a man of probity." Diderot's philosopher demonstrates a tolerance and civility worthy of his distinguished hostess: "Religion, which has made, makes, and will make so many people wicked, has made you still better; you do well to keep it" (*O.p.*, 540).

This was the portrait of the philosopher exercising his métier which Diderot wished to display before the public. Having withdrawn the promise to his brother, he felt personally free to criticize religion; but to avoid unpleasant interviews with the Lieutenant-General of the Paris police, he arranged for the dialogue to be attributed to an Italian writer, Thomas Crudeli. Yet in spite of the complex flummery surrounding its publication, the work was recognized as Diderot's.[8] If he still needed to use discretion when publishing, he no longer felt obliged to hide his manuscripts in a drawer. Diderot had found his voice; he was the judge of others and no longer the judged. The rest of humanity might need the presence of an onlooker; like so many children they craved and feared the father's regard. But Diderot was the father; he had paid full price for his paternal status and considered the philosopher he had created the ethical superior of the Christian God. "I permit everyone to think in his own way," he grandly informs the Maréchale, one of those still living under the watchful eye of the Great Spectator. "For you it is sweet to imagine, next to you, over your head, a great and powerful being, who sees you walk upon the earth, and that idea affirms your step. Continue, Madame, to enjoy this august guarantor of your thoughts, this spectator, this sublime model of your actions" (*O.p.*, 540). Diderot had made the same observation to the Tsarina: "Your Majesty wants a great spectator who bends down toward the earth and watches her walk. She imagines high in the sky an approbator worthy of her. As for me, poor creature, I duck and go as if nobody were watching me" (*C.*, XIV, 83).

"Poor creature" as he may have been, Diderot felt self-assured enough to repudiate his earlier espousal of the theory of man's innate virtue in favor of an ethic based solely upon the evaluation of action. In a collection of reflections on Helvétius's magnum opus *De l'homme,* written in 1773, he set forth his view of moral good and evil: "Is man born good or bad? If we can only give the name good to the one who does good, and the name wicked to the one who does evil, surely man, when born, is neither good nor evil" (*A.-T.*, II, 406).

The verb of activity, *faire,* to do or to make, had replaced the verbs of essence, *naître,* to be born, and *être,* to be, thus denying all values not based upon constructive achievement. Viewed in this way, the mighty of the earth and the divinity on high were not by nature better than the most undistinguished human being. In fact, if they failed to utilize their greater power to do good, they were infinitely worse. Hence, for Diderot, if the Christian God existed, he would be scarcely superior to the flagrantly derelict god of the pagans:

Jupiter sits down at the table; he jokes with his wife, makes suggestive remarks to Venus, watches Hebe tenderly, slaps Ganymede on the buttocks, has his cup filled. As he drinks, the sound of cries from the different parts of the earth reaches his ears, the noise grows louder. He gets up impatiently, opens the door of the celestial vault and says: "Plague in Asia, war in Europe, famine in

Africa, here a frost, there a storm, somewhere else a volcano. . . ."
Then he shuts his trap door, sits back down at the table, gets
drunk, goes to bed, sleeps, and he calls that governing the world.
(*A.-T.*, II, 450)

The divinity, like the rest of creation, should be judged on its
actions, and even leaving aside the loutish amusements described by no less an authority than Homer, the most chari-
table view to be taken of an omnipotent God was that he did
not exist. "One of Jupiter's representatives on earth [Louis
XIV] gets up, makes his own coffee or chocolate, signs orders
without reading them, orders a [sedan] chair, comes back
from the forest, undresses, sits down at the table, gets drunk
like Jupiter or like a porter, goes to sleep on the same pillow
as his mistress, and he calls that governing his empire" (*A.-T.*,
II, 450).

Diderot felt that the years he had spent doing what he considered right, rendering services to people for whom he had
no particular respect or fondness, had put him in the position
to judge others at the same time that it freed him from their
judgment.

6/The Trickster's Turn

In his *Eloge de Richardson*, written in 1761, Diderot had stated his belief that the role of the artist was Messianic, his function to lead men to virtue. Since mankind was essentially good, the artist needed to tap those springs of innate sympathy which had been silted over by the processes of civilization and purification would well up from within. To effect this salutary process the artist should depict innocence being persecuted in a way to cause the reader to identify with those who suffer (*O.e.*, 33).

But now, some ten years later, Diderot's attitude toward man's inner nature had undergone a radical revision. His recognition of the amoral forces of the instincts led him to envision a world in which "those who act and those who suffer" are equally pursuing their own ends. In *Ceci n'est pas un conte*, another of the dialogues in which real persons and events are depicted, Diderot portrays the pitiful Mlle de La Chaux, dying destitute after being exploited and then abandoned by the cynical Gardeil, as sharing equal responsibility for her fate with her lover. Diderot presents a conversation between himself and a somewhat literal-minded interlocutor in which they discuss La Chaux's misfortunes. The interlocutor asks what Chaux found in the abominable Gardeil to justify her sacrifices. Diderot reminds him that he too had once been sexually enthralled by an otherwise worthless person. "Mlle de La Chaux, the honest, sensitive Mlle de La Chaux promised herself secretly, from instinct, without being aware of it, the happiness which you knew, which made you say of [your mistress]: 'If that miserable creature, that wretch, insists on rejecting me I will take a pistol and blow my brains out in her foyer'" (*O.r.*, 801).

If the nun Suzanne Simonin, so pure that her "chastity must have been miraculously preserved by an act of Providence," had been Diderot's ideal heroine in his Richardsonian days, Mlle de La Chaux, whom Diderot describes as having failed to take advantage of Mme de Pompadour's offer of a pension, offering pretext after pretext, and thus "twice missed the chance to pull herself out of her distress" (*O.r.*, 811), embodied his view of the more typical human situation in his later years. In reality, as opposed to the novel, people could not be divided into tyrants and victims, so many Lovelaces and Clarissas. The person who was exploited in one relationship might dominate in another, like La Chaux herself, who after being immolated to Gardeil goes on coolly to take advantage of devoted Dr. Le Camus. Or he who shows absolute probity in one area of his life might behave atrociously under different circumstances.

If this were the case, what was to be the tactic of the philosopher as artist, if he wished "to lead men to virtue"? To depict innocence being persecuted only pandered to the reader's taste for scenes which were, at bottom, erotic, letting him enjoy titillation while still feeling virtuous. If he wept over the pathos, he shed marvelously warm and pleasurable tears, which served, in Diderot's words, "more to light the fires than to extinguish them. If one bemoans misfortunes and torments, it is to excite desire and not repentance."

The work of the artist should not consist of stimulating and elaborating the fantasies of the reader in such a way that he could gratify his instincts while continuing to consider himself innocent. The author's true obligation, if he wished to help men to find a surer basis of morality, lay in forcing the reader inward; to an examination of his own inadmissable and frequently childish desires. Only by becoming aware of his inner wishes and unformulated expectations could man free himself from their silent domination and behave as a reasonable being. Where Rousseau and Voltaire, each in his own way, were intent on combating the "prejudices of society" and the "superstitions of the masses," Diderot turned his attention to the misconceptions he saw as equally pernicious, those held by the individual about himself.

It should not be inferred from this insistence on the value of self-knowledge that Diderot somehow prefigured modern psychoanalytic theorists. It was not the depths of the unconscious, the *terra incognita* of the repressed, which he had found in himself or which he wished other men to discover. Diderot felt that the area which needed exploration was directly adjacent to the most public and conscious part of the mind, as a slum abuts a grand boulevard. He was not advocating intrepid plunges into the jungles of New Guinea, only an occasional stroll through the less attractive parts of town.

Jacques le fataliste, a novel-length, highly unconventional narration, mostly written during Diderot's trip to Russia, is generally considered his masterpiece. The two central characters are the "Author" and the "Reader," and their relationship is far from the sentimental honeymoon Diderot had idealized in the *Eloge.* They are involved in an antagonistic commerce, each wanting something from the other, each unwilling to give what is being demanded. Since a book cannot exist, however, without the participation of both, some kind of uneasy balance must be maintained.

The "author's" desires are relatively straightforward; he wishes to prattle on endlessly, following his own train of thought with no regard for his audience, and have his every word devoured with delight. His most unclear, repetitive, meandering phrases should be prized by the "reader" as so many jewels of literary expression.

The "reader," on the other hand, wants to hear some interesting tales about sex and violence, concerning characters whom he can embrace as virtuous or detest as evil. The narration should go along at just the right pace: neither so quickly that the scenes cannot develop adequately in his mind nor so slowly that he gets bored. It should be presented in a realistic way, to heighten the illusion, and be written in an elegant and literate style, to flatter the "reader's" picture of himself as a man of taste. The book should offer him what life too frequently lacks —effortless gratification of instinctual wishes with no impingement upon his self-respect.

The two secondary characters, or main-characters-once-removed, are also pitted against one another in a power struggle that mirrors the one between the "author" and the "reader." Jacques, a servant, wishes to speak and needs to be listened to; the trauma of his childhood was being gagged into silence by his grandfather. The master, on the other hand, is a rather passive, vacant gentleman who craves Jacques's incessant chatter because it keeps him from falling into a mindless torpor. "You don't know this guy yet," says Diderot, "he has eyes like you or me but most of the time you cannot tell if he is looking. He does not sleep nor does he stay awake, he lets himself exist: that is his habitual function" (*O.r.*, 515).

The story of Jacques's loves is at once the central "subject" of their conversation and the "object" of the struggle between them. The master would like to hear the story recounted in an energetic and comprehensible way, leading to an interesting description of consummation. But he is a greedy master, like the Sultan in *Les Bijoux indiscrets;* he wants the stories to go on and on.

Jacques resists coming directly to the point; he is aware that he has only a limited number of anecdotes to tell and refuses to repeat himself: "Monsieur is preparing the saddest future for me. What will become of me when I have nothing more to say?" The two struggles become intertwined in the book, often the "reader's" interest and the master's are identical; they both want to hear the story of Jacques's loves. But when the account becomes hopelessly fragmented by frequent interruptions or Jacques's digressions, the "reader" and the master, both faithful only to their curiosity, are prepared to abandon Jacques altogether and follow a more promising raconteur. Such is the hostess at the inn where they spend the night, who begins a tale about Mme de la Pommeraye and the Marquis d'Arcis in a pleasingly professional way, only to be herself interrupted. Diderot proposes that the "reader" decide the direction of the narration himself: who offers the better chance of hearing a good story, Jacques or the hostess? "Speak frankly, reader, do you want us to quit this elegant and prolix chatterbox of a hostess and take up the loves of Jacques again? As for me, it doesn't make any difference" (*O.r.*, 604).

The hostess's story, a complete and conventionally told tale, sits in the middle of the novel, preceded and followed by fragmented anecdotes and scraps of interrupted dialogue, like a mountain rising from a sea strewn with reefs. After the travelers leave her inn, the master and the "reader" increase their demands to hear Jacques's loves recounted. The "author" points out that the "reader's" erotic curiosity is insatiable.

Now then, reader, always love stories, one, two, three love stories I have told you, three or four more love stories still to come; that's a lot of love stories. On the other hand, it is true that since I am writing for you I must either get along without your applause or serve you according to your taste, and your taste is fixed on love stories. All your fiction, in verse or in prose, is love stories; almost all your poems, elegies, epilogues, idylls, songs, epistles, comedies, tragedies, operas are love stories. Almost all your paintings and statues are nothing but love stories. You have been nourished exclusively on love stories your entire life and you never get sick of them. You have been held to this diet and you will continue to be held to it; men and women, big children and small, without tiring of it. To tell the truth, it is marvelous. (*O.r.*, 671–72)

But the mood of the "author" appears to grow more somber as the narration continues. The master, tiring of Jacques's evasions, asks frankly to hear how his servant lost his virginity, confiding: "I have always been partial to accounts of that great event" (*O.r.*, 690). Jacques starts to describe his early sexual experiences. The first one is amusing but disquieting. Jacques had, in effect, forced a girl who meant nothing to him to have relations with him; "love" is a tenuous euphemism for what is essentially rape. His second adventure and his third descend several notches from the first; gaiety is soon displaced by vulgarity; and the fourth anecdote is obscene without redeeming social value. Diderot's "reader," his thirst for gross details temporarily slaked, turns on the "author" indignantly: "How can a sensible man, who has morals, who prides himself on being a philosopher, amuse himself spouting such obscene tales?" "First of all," says Diderot, at last avenging himself upon the public which had claimed to be scandalized by *Les Bijoux indiscrets*, "these are not tales, this is a history, and I do not feel any more guilty, and perhaps less, when I write the follies of Jacques, than Suetonius when he transcribed the debauchery of Tiberius. Why is it you have indulgence only for the dead? If you reflected a bit on that partiality you would see that it springs from some vicious principle. If you are innocent you will not read me, if you are corrupt you will read me without consequence" (*O.r.*, 714).

The more the "author" considers the "reader's" attitude, the more incensed he becomes: "I enjoy myself writing the foolishness you do, your follies make me laugh, my account makes you angry. Reader, to speak frankly, I find that the more wicked of us two is not I. Vile hypocrites! Leave me in peace. F . . . like unbridled asses, but permit me to say f. . . . I pardon you the action, you pardon me the word. You bravely pronounce, kill, steal, betray, and the other you would not dare utter aloud? Is it that the fewer of these so-called impurities you exhale in words, the more stay in your thoughts?" (*O.r.*, 714–15).

The narration terminates with the story of Jacques's loves, that is, the description of his seduction of Denise, when he was arrested with his hand on his girl's kneecap. The master is persuaded that he will not have to wait much longer, for "when one has gotten to the knee there is not much road left to travel." "My master," says Jacques tranquilly, "Denise has a longer thigh than most." The story of Jacques's loves will have to remain unfinished. "I see, reader," says the "author," "that this makes you angry. Very well, take up the story yourself and continue it according to your fantasy" (*O.r.*, 773–74, 777).

Diderot's purpose in employing these unorthodox tactics was not simply to frustrate and humiliate his public, but rather to forge a new relationship with it, based on shared lucidity. By spelling out the unspoken conventions implicit in the novel as an established form, Diderot hoped to bring the public to a fuller awareness of its own mental life. The old contract between "author" and "reader" served only to enmesh them in a demeaning ritual, catering to man's constant desire to enjoy "the pleasures of vice and the honors of virtue." The new contract would offer them both the possibility of liberation, not from the pressure of the instincts but from the debasing hypocrisy surrounding their expression.

The rationalized commerce between the "author" and the "reader" had its paradigm in Jacques's plan to place his relationship with the master on a reasonable basis. Convention dictated that the master be morally and intellectually superior to the valet. Nature, in this instance, had clearly decreed otherwise: Jacques and his master both recognized that of the two, the valet was the better man. Jacques's native superiority was the tacit foundation of their understanding. But when the master learns that Jacques's mistress is Denise, a servant girl whom he had tried in vain to seduce, he asserts his social superiority in order to humiliate his successful rival.

"The hussy! To prefer a Jacques!" ["Jacques" in French is a generic term for peasant.]
"A Jacques! A Jacques, sir, is a man like any other."
"Jacques, you are wrong. A Jacques is not a man like any other."
"Sometimes better than another."
"Jacques, you are forgetting yourself. Go back to the story of your loves and remember that you are not and will never be anything but a Jacques."

The ensuing violent quarrel is eventually terminated by the hostess at the inn. Jacques proposes that they draw up a "reasonable arrangement" to prevent all future arguments over the same issue.

"Let us stipulate, number one, since it is written on high that I be essential to you, and that I feel, I know, that you cannot get along without me, I will use these advantages whenever and as often as the occasion presents itself."
"But Jacques," the master replies, "nobody has ever stipulated such a thing."
"Number two: since it is as impossible for Jacques to be unaware of his ascendancy and his power over his master as it is for his master to misapprehend his own weakness and rid himself

of his indulgence, it is necessary that Jacques be insolent and, to keep the peace, that his master not notice. It was decided [by nature] that you would have the title and I would have the thing itself. If you attempted to oppose the will of nature, you would be wasting your time."

"What difference does our consent make to a law of nature?" asks the master.

"A great deal. Do you think it is useless to know, once and for all, absolutely, clearly, how we are to consider ourselves?" (*O.r.*, 664–66)

The weight of the argument is adaptive, not revolutionary. Diderot was not especially castigating the society which reversed the order of nature; on the contrary, Jacques and his master appear to enjoy a mutually satisfactory relationship, each getting something he needs from the other. The source of the quarrels that disturb their accord is the refusal to accept the price which has to be paid for the satisfactions each enjoys.

The fabric of the novel, as it weaves itself within the framework of the two sets of relationships, presents an elaborate, dense, and frequently patternless surface. The "reader" expects the novelist to arrange events in such a way that they form an intelligible design. Unlike real life, in which experience is confusing and fragmented, the novel should offer incidents which may at first appear unrelated but eventually are shown to be part of a comprehensible totality. The "reader" craves intellectual closure, his *amour-propre* is offended by constant bafflement. Hence, if the artist's métier is to give the public the occasion to feel what it wishes to feel, his role is to arrange literature to be more intellectually satisfying than life.[1]

But, as we saw in the *Paradoxe sur le comédien,* Diderot's concern with his picture of himself as a philosopher, as a man who led other men to virtue, could not permit him to be satisfied with serving as a mere pander to public taste. His function was rather to force the reader into recognizing the existence of such wishes, a recognition which the traditional novelist was at great pains to spare his reader.

A woman is observed falling from a horse. In the real world this is a frustrating experience for the spectator; it interests him but he does not know what to think about it. Why did she fall? Who is she? What happens to her as a consequence? He loses sight of her as a crowd gathers and mulls it over until the next arresting but incomprehensible event occurs. His curiosity is repeatedly aroused and seldom satisfied by his daily perceptions. What is worse, he has nothing definitive to tell anybody, and, like Jacques, he has a mania for talking, because "it draws [him] from his abject state, places him on the rostrum, transforms him suddenly into an interesting personage. He goes to the Place de Grève [where executions take place] to find a scene he can recount when he gets back to his neighborhood, this scene or that, he doesn't care, provided that he play a role, gather together the neighbors, be listened to" (*O.r.*, 669–70).

This is the great advantage of fiction over reality. When the heroine of Marivaux's novel *La Vie de Marianne* falls leaving church, the accident permits her ankle to be glimpsed by a handsome young nobleman who happens to be the nephew of her protector. The circumstances are "artfully allied" and, while romantic, not implausible.

Diderot has a woman fall off a horse, revealing not just her ankle but her whole backside. "What I couldn't do with this adventure if I took it into my head to exasperate you! I would give this woman some importance; I would make her the niece of the village *curé* [as was Marivaux's heroine]. I would excite the peasants of the village, I would prepare rivalries and passions because this peasant girl was, after all, beautiful beneath her petticoats. Jacques and his master would have noticed, love has been aroused upon less seductive occasions" (*O.r.*, 496).

It is up to the reader: he may choose to hear more about the woman who fell from the horse, or the story of Jacques's loves. "Once and for all," Diderot asks, "explain yourself. Would that make you happy or not? If it would, let us put the peasant girl back on the horse, behind the rider, let them go, and return to our two voyagers." Diderot adjusts the doses of stimulation and frustration adroitly, so that the reader who begins to lose himself in the fantasy being unwound for him is again and again caught up short by the "author's" insistence on exposing the mechanisms of fiction and those of his own expectations.

For if art is to lead men to be virtuous in their lives and not just in their imaginations, it must penetrate the special mental set employed in apprehending art and reach the levels of the personality where reality is perceived.

Traditional fiction does for the reader what traditional religion does for mankind at large: it imposes an intelligent order upon the chaos of experience. Random phenomena do not appear incomprehensible to the believer because he is enlightened as to the secret design of the universe. Superstition survives because we would rather heed an ominous warning than face a universe totally devoid of personal significance. The common run of men share with Catherine of Russia and the Maréchale de xxx the need for a great intelligence in the sky that lends meaning to existence.

Jacques insists on many occasions throughout the novel that all events are "written on high," on a "great scroll." The "great scroll" implies a Great Author, and Jacques finds both comfort and a source of pride in considering his life so prerecorded. "Thou who made the great scroll," Jacques prays, "whatever thou art, whose fingers traced the writing which is on high, thou hast always known what I needed, let thy will be done."

"Wouldn't you do just as well to be quiet?" asks the master.

"Maybe yes, maybe no. I pray at random, and whatever happens I would not rejoice or complain if I could control myself, but I am so inconsistent and violent that I forget my principles and I laugh and cry like a fool" (*O.r.*, 656).

For behavior is not much influenced by principles, as Diderot demonstrated in the *Entretien d'un philosophe* . . . , or to put it another way, we believe what flatters our vanity, we do what makes us happy. The anecdotes in the novel repeatedly contradict Jacques's assertion.[2] There is no need to invoke fatality to explain why any of the events take place. The characters in the stories are far from passive toys of destiny; they are impassioned architects of their fates and those of others.[3] Victims in the stories fall prey to other people with stronger wills or cleverer minds, not to the machinations of some ultimate author.

The episode of Mme de la Pommeraye, the longest and most complete in the work, illustrates the irrelevance of Jacques's "principle." Mme de la Pommeraye decides to avenge herself upon her lover, the Marquis d'Arcis, for having tired of her. She arranges for him to meet a beautiful young woman, in reality a prostitute, whom she introduces as a pious recluse. The Marquis, so self-infatuated that he cannot recognize his former mistress's spleen, falls into the trap set for him. Mme de la Pommeraye stage-manages the whole affair, tantalizing the Marquis to the point where he marries the chippy in disguise. The day after his wedding Mme de la Pommeraye takes her revenge: she informs him of his new bride's former profession. After an interval of soul-searching the Marquis returns to his wife and forgives her for her past. They settle down to a marriage which turns out to be, on the whole, better than most, illustrating Diderot's notion that a well-developed technical virtue is often to be preferred to the best of intentions.

The tale differs markedly from the run of eighteenth-century fiction in that nothing happens by chance, there are no fortuitous meetings, remarkable coincidences, or providential interventions; each event takes place because one of the characters wanted it to. Actions turn out to have unpredicted consequences only because the active party, subject to his own passions, miscalculates. The Marquis deludes himself when he thinks that his yawns and sighs of boredom go unnoticed by Mme de la Pommeraye. She, in turn, sees him as being more rigid and hidebound than he really is, and the former streetwalker shows greater presence of mind in throwing herself upon her husband's mercy than she has been credited with.

Human capacities for good and for evil are not fixed and measurable quantities, they are knowable only as they are realized through action. For Diderot, man's acts were his fate. To the extent that he acted well his life would be happy, but in order to act well he needed to divest himself of his prejudices and see reality as clearly as he could. In *Jacques le fataliste* the philosopher presented the antithesis of a traditional novel, a program to lead the reader away from illusion toward greater awareness of his own mental processes.

7/The Final Accounting

The Enlightenment was virtually unanimous in echoing Aristotle's premise of the *Nichomachean Ethics* that the objective of all human activity must be happiness. The belief was shared by the pious, like Bossuet, who held that "the whole purpose of man is to be happy," and the atheists, like d'Holbach, who took it as axiomatic that man acted "in order to render his existence happy." [1] Agreement ceased at this point, however, in eighteenth-century France as well as in fourth-century Athens. For Bossuet is was "Jesus Christ [who] came to show us the way," while for d'Holbach reason was the only infallible guide to happiness. Rousseau claimed that real, authentic happiness was a state of total self-absorption, in which "time has no meaning, where the present lasts forever, with no other feeling of pain or pleasure, desire or fear than that of our existence."

If Diderot never stopped believing that the best way for him to be happy was in trying to be virtuous, he abandoned the attempt to prove that his belief was logically binding for others. His need to order his life upon intellectually irrefutable syllogisms had weakened. His own obsession with virtue seemed to him more and more just another quirk of human nature, a peculiarity difficult to impose upon the species as a whole. As he acknowledges to the Maréchale in *L' Entretien d'un philosophe* . . . , if believers were inconsistent because they heeded their passions more than their faith, he too was inconsistent when he adhered to an idealistic code contradicting both his reason and his desires. While he resolved *how* he should behave in order to be virtuous, he had by no means found an adequate explanation of *why* he should bother himself to be virtuous. For society, on one hand, was no longer "a divinity on earth" as it had appeared to him when he began work on the *Encyclopédie,* but had come to seem like a machine in which men were only springs, "moving, reacting against one another, endlessly fatigued, more of them broken in a day than in a year under the anarchy of nature" (*O.p.,* 512). And, on the other hand, if society offered no real imperative to be virtuous, nature, "Man's constant enemy" (*C.,* XIII, 92), had nothing to say about his duties either except "be happy."

In his refutation of Helvétius's book *De l'homme,* in which the author attempted to prove that all men were born with equal mental and moral capacities, Diderot warned of the dangers in attempting to demonstrate the undemonstrable, of trying to provide proof of what was only an emotional conviction. Helvétius claimed that the average man was born a blank, capable of being inscribed with any talents. Diderot, respecting the goodness of heart which lay behind such an egalitarian position, nevertheless wished to remind his friend that the most sincerely held notions can only impress others if they are buttressed by rational arguments and compelling appeals to experience.

Believe that, Helvétius, if it suits you; but realize that you are banging your head uselessly, as I have done, on questions which you will never fathom. I mention myself because I am conscious of my efforts and acquainted with my stubbornness. I have been unable to find the truth, and I sought it with more qualities than you demand. I will go further: if there are seemingly complex questions which turned out, upon examination, to be simple, there are seemingly simple ones which I judged beyond my grasp. For example, I am convinced, that even in a society as badly regulated as ours, where the vice which succeeds is often applauded and the virtue which fails almost always ridiculous, I am convinced, I say, that all in all, the best thing to do for one's happiness is to be a good man: in my opinion that is the most important and interesting work to be done, that is the one I shall remember with the greatest satisfaction in my last moments. It is a question which I have meditated a hundred times with all the force of mind of which I am capable; I had, I believe, the necessary gifts, shall I confess it? I did not even dare take up the pen to write the first line. I said to myself: "If I do not emerge victorious from this engagement, I become the apologist for wickedness; I shall have betrayed the cause of virtue, I shall have encouraged man to vice." No, I feel I am inadequate to this sublime task. (A.-T., II, 344–45)

The inadequacy which Diderot complained of, however, was rooted less in an intellectual failure to come to grips with the problem than in his evasion of a fundamental issue within himself. It was true that he spent a great deal of time and energy rendering services for other people, doing good in a multitude of little ways that caused his more cynical friends like Grimm to refer to him condescendingly as the wastrel of his own gifts. But had he been motivated exclusively by an ineluctable "taste for virtue" every time he got involved in someone else's affairs? Was the pleasure he took in resolving other people's difficulties purely the glow cast by the good deed?

Between 1770 and 1781 Diderot produced at least three versions of a curious play, centering around a character named M. Hardouin, an undisguised representation of the philosopher himself. Each successive portrayal of M. Hardouin was a more subtle and nuanced study of the multiple motives that impelled him to become the unofficial *ombudsman* for half of Paris. In *Est-il bon? Est-il méchant?*, as the play was definitively titled, M. Hardouin devotes his days to serving other people's causes. Like Diderot's father in Langres, he is "the friend of all the unfortunate," besieged by friends, acquaintances, and even strangers who do not hesitate to enlist him in their causes. He has become so widely known that one of the characters in the play, M. de Crancey, complains: "I had a devil of a time getting in to see you, it's worse than at a minister's office or his assistant's. Do you realize I have been foaming with rage in your waiting room for two hours?" (*A.-T.*, VIII, 176). During the course of the comedy, a Mme de Chépy arrogantly demands that he write a little play for her friend's birthday celebration; Mme Bertrand, a widow, begs him to persuade a government official to grant a pension to her son; M. de Crancey wants him to convince the mother of the girl he loves that they should be married; and M. Hardouin is charged with half a dozen other commissions as well. "I give [my time and my talent] to all those who think enough of them to accept them," he remarks.

He is marvelously adroit at managing other people's affairs. Within the day he has brought all of the issues to successful conclusion by a series of cleverly unscrupulous maneuvers. He agrees to write the *divertissement* for Mme de Chépy only upon the request of her pretty servant, humiliating the mistress in her own eyes and those of her maid. He procures the pension for the widow Bertrand's son by implying that the boy was probably his own bastard son when he importunes his friend the Minister. Mme de Vertillac is induced to give her daughter permission, in writing, to marry Crancey when M. Hardouin makes it appear that the girl is pregnant, reminding the mother that her own wedding had taken place a bit later than the event it was supposed to sanctify. At the end of the play, each of the characters has received what he wanted but at the price of a blow to his self-esteem. In each case the humiliation is more or less justified, but a certain residue of subdued resentment nevertheless taints the pleasurable denouement.

Just as Diderot the "author" exercised his technical skill as artist to tease and manipulate the "reader" in *Jacques le fataliste*, M. Hardouin applies the same talent to managing the other characters in *Est-il bon? Est-il méchant?* In *Jacques*, Diderot justified his assaults upon the reader's dignity by the salutary moral results which they were supposed to produce. Though the goodness of the philosopher caused him to behave cruelly as an artist, his ultimate goal was to lead men to virtue. Now, however, toward the end of his life, Diderot finally gave voice to the other side of the taste for persiflage that had deceived M. de Croismare and so many others through the years. Like the Sultan in *Les Bijoux indiscrets*, he took pleasure in pulling the strings which made other people jump, a pleasure having very little to do with virtue. Answering the rhetorical question he had posed in the *Eloge de Richardson*, "Who would wish to be Lovelace with all of his advantages?" he proclaimed that he, Diderot, would! "Me, they say I am a good man! I am not a good man at all. I was born fundamentally hard, wicked, perverse. I am touched almost to tears by the tenderness of this mother [Mme Bertrand] for her child, by her sensitivity, her gratitude. I even find her to my taste, and in spite of myself I persist in a project which will perhaps devastate her. . . . Hardouin, you are amused by everything, there is nothing sacred for you, you are an out-and-out monster" (*A.-T.*, VIII, 202).

M. Hardouin performs acts which on balance seem more beneficial than harmful, from motives which, by and large, are more vicious than generous. Diderot came to see his own need for virtue not as a mysterious gift of the gods but as a compromise permitting him the pleasure of seeing people suffer while satisfying his conscience. He compensated for the excitement he experienced in watching a pretty woman weep by helping her out of her trouble; the perversity of his enjoyment was balanced by the efficacity of his deeds.

In a letter to an unnamed correspondent,[2] Diderot reflected upon an incident of his childhood which had made a deep impression on him. "The more I examine myself, the more I am convinced that in our youth there comes a moment which is decisive for our character. A little girl, as pretty as a heart, bit me on the hand. When I complained to her father he pulled up her dress before me, and that little rump stayed in my mind and will stay there as long as I live. Who knows its influence on my morals?" (*C.*, XVI, 64).

His memory of the little bottom being paddled may have been triggered by Rousseau's readings from the *Confessions*,[3] where he attributed his own sexual inclinations to a boyhood spanking he had received from his cousin, Mlle Lambercier: "I found this punishment less terrible in reality than in expectation . . . for I had discovered mixed in the pain, in the shame even, a sensuality leaving me more desirous than fearful of experiencing it again. Who would believe that this punishment, received by an eight-year-old from a woman of thirty, decided my tastes, my desires, my passions, my very self for the rest of my life?" (*O.c.*, I, 15). For Diderot as for Rousseau, the discovery was made that a long-ago spanking had been the occasion of pleasurable sensation. Rousseau, the victim of the punishment, sought unsuccessfully to replicate the scene. He described how, as a youth, he used to bare his buttocks in a courtyard where young girls came to draw water, hoping in vain for at least a passing slap. Unable to communicate his desire to be spanked into arousal by a willing woman, he had to convert it into a moral equivalent. "Never daring to declare my taste, I flattered it at least by means of situations which maintained the idea. To kneel before an imperious mistress, to obey her orders, to beg her forgiveness, these were very sweet pleasures for me, and the more my lively imagination fired my blood, the more I resembled an enthralled lover" (*O.c.*, I, 17).

Diderot expressed under several different guises the stimulation of observing another person suffer. At the beginning of his "project of sincerity," he was wont to attribute this to some purely aesthetic peculiarity of the human mind: "The great effects are always born of voluptuous ideas interlaced with terrible ones," he wrote Sophie in 1762. "For example, beautiful, half-nude women who present us with delicious drinks in the bloody skulls of our enemies. That is the model of all sublime things. This is when the soul opens to pleasure and shivers with horror" (*C.*, IV, 196). But in *La Religieuse*, Diderot depicted the association between pity and sexual stimulation more explicitly. The lesbian Mother Superior is shown begging Suzanne to recount her persecutions: " 'Tell, my child,' " she implores. " 'I am waiting, I am feeling the most imperative need to be moved. . . .' " She reacts to the young nun's descriptions of her sufferings with increasing excitement: " 'The cruel creatures! To squeeze these arms with ropes!' And she took my arms and kissed them. 'To drench those eyes with tears!' And she kissed them. 'To force a moan from that mouth!' And she kissed it. 'To dare to circle this throat with a cord, to prick these shoulders with sharp points!' And she drew my linen from my neck and head, she opened the top of my dress, my hair hung thick on my bare shoulders, my bosom was partially nude, and she showered kisses on my neck, my bare shoulders, and my half-uncovered bosom" (*O.r.*, 348).

By 1767 Diderot had come to recognize that he himself took pleasure in the fantasy of sympathy seeded with lubricity. In point of fact, to Diderot the role of protector of a beloved woman in danger was seductive enough to warrant putting her there. "Who will not wish to see his mistress encircled with flames, if he can promise himself to rush into them like

Alcibiades and carry her off in his arms? It is a beautiful spectacle, that of virtue undergoing great persecution, the most terrible attacks against virtue do not displease us" (*A.-T.*, XI, 143).

In the case of both Diderot and Rousseau, dredging up the childhood memories of pleasure associated with spanking had assumed a moral value independent of the events recalled or the emotions connected with them. The exploration of the self—before the world for Rousseau, or for one person's eyes alone, as in Diderot's case—acquired a significance quite apart from the discoveries made. It was the sign of a virtue outweighing whatever transgression might be revealed. Rousseau, at the very end of the *Confessions,* declared that his attempt at sincerity had succeeded; despite the unworthy acts to which he had admitted in the work, or, rather, because of these very admissions, he had become worthy to judge his accusers and even to sentence them: "For my part I state aloud and without fear: whoever will examine with his own eyes my nature, my character, my morals [etc.], and can believe I am a dishonest man, is himself fit to be hanged" (*O.c.,* I, 656).

Diderot also believed that the voyage into the self had a value greater than could be nullifed by the shameful memories exhumed. But his conclusion was different from Rousseau's: rather than insisting that any critic of his character was himself a likely candidate for the noose, Diderot summarized his feelings in a sober statement of the generality of human moral mediocrity: "The assiduous examination of the self serves less to improve us than to teach us that neither we nor anybody else is very good" (*C.,* V, 228).

"Is he good? Is he bad?" asks the befuddled Mme de Chépy at the end of the play. "First one, then the other," her servant answers. "Like you, like me, like everybody," rejoins a third victim-beneficiary (*A.-T.*, VIII, 244). Diderot had told Sophie ruefully, near the beginning of his self-exploration, "At the bottom of our most tender passions and noblest sentiments, there is a hint of testicle" (*C.*, III, 216). More than twenty years later, Diderot saw that the sexual motives behind men's actions were not shameful but inevitable and ultimately even productive. People needed the impulsion of their erotic wishes in order to accomplish anything of value in the world: "Each man must couple with the muse who suits him, she with whom he experiences himself and finds himself: he is nothing with the others or has only a false erection: he will love them badly" (*A.-T.*, II, 293).

In 1780 and 1781, while he was finishing the play about M. Hardouin's malice in charity, Diderot decided to return to the great novel of innocence persecuted he had written twenty years earlier, *La Religieuse*. He revised it for publication in the *Correspondance littéraire*, adding two parts, a Post-scriptum to the memoir itself, and a document which has come to be called the "Préface-annexe."

The Post-scriptum was designed to focus attention on the "bit of testicle" implicitly present in the memoir. Throughout the long letter the nun writes to M. de Croismare, the gentleman who was "to take charge of her destiny," she emphasizes her complete innocence while describing, in scene after scene, the sexual interest which she arouses in others. In 1782, Diderot added the following note as a last paragraph to her memoir:

These memoirs, which I wrote in haste, I just reread in a calmer state of mind, and I noticed that without having in the least intended to, I showed myself as unhappy as I really am but a great deal more attractive. Would it be that we believe men less susceptible to the tale of our suffering than to the picture of our charms? And that it would seem easier to seduce them than to engage their sympathies? I know men too little, nor have I studied myself enough to have the answer. However, if the Marquis, to whom everyone attributes the most delicate taste, were persuaded that it was not to his charity but to his vice that I was addressing myself, what would he think of me? This reflection troubles me. To tell the truth, he would be wrong to impute to me personally an instinct common to my entire sex. I am a woman, perhaps a bit of a flirt, what can I say? (*O.r.*, 392–93)

Suzanne has aged twenty years in a few minutes. From the girl so pure that she couldn't remember what a lesbian was even after she was told, she has come to join the human race; she too does her steps in the "vile pantomime" which is the "great jog of the world."

The "Préface-annexe" was ostensibly merely a reproduction of Grimm's reminiscences, which had appeared in the *Correspondance littéraire* in 1770, of the cruel hoax that he and Diderot had perpetrated upon M. de Croismare.[4] Grimm had described the "vile plot" and published the fraudulent letters of the pseudo-nun and the authentic answers of the honest Marquis. He mentioned that Diderot had begun to compose a sort of long memoir, or novel, detailing the struggles of Sister Suzanne, but that this work had never been finished. Diderot now took Grimm's account and reworked it, adding a note here and an anecdote there, calling the document thus produced "a useful preface if there ever was one." The "Préface-annexe" describes how the conspirators passed their time "reading amidst bursts of laughter, the letters which were supposed to make our good Marquis weep, and we read, with the same burst of laughter, the honest answers of our worthy and generous friend" (*O.r.*, 850). By juxtaposing the beautifully wrought literary illusion of the persecuted nun with the blunt facts of the plot against M. de Croismare, Diderot made it clear that the victim in reality was not the nun being abused by a vicious society, but the Marquis, being had by his perverse friends.

The effect of reading the two parts together is disconcerting. The reader, who has been induced to identify with the suffering Sister Suzanne against her oppressors, realizes, in reading the "Préface-annexe," that he, along with M. de Croismare, has been gulled by an author who was snickering at the most pathetic scenes in the novel. As in *Jacques le fataliste*, which Diderot revised for publication at the same time, the "author" deliberately destroys the reader's pleasure in losing himself in a dream world by forcing him to recognize it as such. Through Jacques, however, the "author" addresses the "reader" directly, pointing out the artifice of even the most realistic fiction; in *La Religieuse*, Diderot removes himself from the scene and lets the documents speak for themselves. The didactic purpose was better served if the reader were to draw his own conclusions. As Diderot remarked in his refutation of Helvétius's *De l'homme*, written after *Jacques le fataliste*: "A paradoxical author must never state his idea, but always his proofs: he must enter the soul of his reader furtively, not by brute force" (*A.-T.*, II, 272).

Many of the readers of *La Religieuse* were sorry they let Diderot enter their souls at all. Reaction to the simultaneous publication of the touching memoir and the cynical "Préface-annexe" was disapproving and even indignant, as exemplified by M. A.-V. Arnault, who felt that "the reader, disenchanted, almost regrets his initial sympathy. . . . He quickly abandons this correspondence to chase after his sweet illusions," [5] a reaction which would probably have neither pleased nor surprised Diderot very much.

Diderot was not content to have *La Religieuse* comprise a moving and realistic memoir of virtue abused, a disquieting Post-scriptum, and a "Préface-annexe" mocking the illusion of the memoir by detailing the hypocritical machinations of the author and his cronies. He also inserted the following anecdote in such a way that it appeared to have been written by Grimm: "One day while Diderot was writing the memoirs of the unfortunate nun, M. d'Alainville, a mutual friend, visited him and found him plunged in grief, his face bathed in tears. 'What is the matter with you?' asked M. d'Alainville, 'just look at you!' 'The matter with me,' M. Diderot answered, 'is that I am heartbroken over a tale I am telling myself'" (*O.r.*, 850).

The "author" weeping over his own creation had become just another character in a novel. He was as untrustworthy as all the others. As Diderot had concluded in the *Salon* of 1767, "the tears we shed on cold paper impress no one, we need live witnesses." D'Alainville was Diderot's witness, according to Grimm's account; only the account itself was fraudulent. Grimm, like everyone else connected with the work, was being euchred.

Diderot, it seemed, had come at last to the end of his idealizations. Grimm was still his friend, but friendship, like all other human relations, was largely a self-serving commerce rather than the spiritual union of two "beautiful souls," as he had insisted for so many years. He no longer saw Grimm as his own substitute for divinity (a role assigned in a letter Diderot wrote to Mme Nicker upon his return from Russia: "When I need support, or a censor, or a panegyrist, or a witness, I go looking for my friend; while you have your eyes turned towards Heaven, I look toward the Rue Anne, or I run there; my fetish is within my grasp" [*C.*, XIV, 76]).

The adoration of Grimm which had endured so many tests finally came to grief on the two rocks of Diderot's last years: Angélique, and the conception of the philosopher. During a dinner party at Angélique's house, Grimm, his chest now jangling with the various medals his princes had pinned on it, proposed a dilemma to the company, one intended to discredit Diderot's friend the Abbé Raynal, who had just published a highly provocative and dangerous work, *L'Histoire des deux Indes*. According to Grimm, Raynal was either mad or cowardly: mad, if he deliberately insulted powerful people in the knowledge that he would be punished; cowardly, if he thought he was safe from reprisals. Diderot reacted with rage. Grimm, in effect, was ridiculing the *philosophes'* pact, discrediting all the martyrs of reason, from Socrates drinking hemlock to Spinoza being trampled underfoot by the congregation at Amsterdam. Grimm had been corrupted by too many years in the antechambers of the rich. "You have gangrene," Diderot told him, "perhaps it has not made enough progress to be incurable. You would need, I believe, a bit of soliloquy. It is not what I have the courage to tell you that will cure you, it is what you will say to yourself." As for Angélique, apparently much impressed by Grimm's paradox, "I thought she had more courage and logic" (*O.p.*, 643), her father said. The man who had clung to his friends with such intensity was now preparing to separate himself from them. "I see with satisfaction," Diderot wrote to his daughter, "all my ties to others being dissolved."

The disillusionment Diderot experienced in his real friendships was partially compensated for by an imaginary one with the great philosopher of a distant time, Seneca. In 1778, the year Rousseau died, Diderot turned his attention back upon his own life, weighing the decisions he had made and the man he had created through his own actions. He undertook to write a life of Seneca and later a defense against the accusations hurled at the Roman philosopher by the critic of the *Année littéraire*, Geoffroy. The first edition of the *Essai sur les Règnes de Claude et de Néron* appeared in 1778, the second in 1782.[6] The apology, however, was more Diderot's than Seneca's, and the accuser less Geoffroy than Rousseau.

In the 1750s, when Rousseau parted company with a whorish world to retire to the enjoyment of his pure self, Diderot had opted to stay in society, slowly and painfully revising the gratifying views he had held of his own virtue. Since his return from Russia, however, he had put himself in a rather anomalous position. While never personally inclined toward luxury, he was avidly ambitious for Angélique and her family. "By the strangest quirk," he wrote to Sartine, then Secretary of the Navy, "although I believe wealth more opposed to happiness than mediocrity, and I accept the latter quite well for myself, I cannot accept it for them; I want them to be rich, yes, Monsieur, very rich!" (C., XIV, 152).

He assiduously courted the powerful, sparing himself no pains in his efforts to secure favorable positions for his son-in-law. At least one of his maneuvers, attempting to secure a monopoly ·for Vandeul from his old friend Turgot, the Controller-General, was so patently unjust that he is reputed to have sent Angélique to ask the intervention of a third party, the count d'Angiviller, because he was too embarrassed to make such an "unphilosophic" request himself. "If the thing had been just," Angélique is supposed to have told d'Angiviller, "my father would not have had recourse to you" (C., XIV, 116).

Attempting to reconcile his role as courtesan of the rich and flatterer of the Russian despot with his picture of himself as an honest philosopher put Diderot in a rather uncomfortable position. What made it all the more painful was that Rousseau, in his public readings of the Confessions, had described Diderot's reaction when Rousseau decided to reject Louis XV's offer of a pension: "He spoke to me of the pension with an ardor I would never have expected from a philosopher concerning such a subject. He did not make a crime of my refusal to be presented to the King, but he made a terrible one of my indifference towards the pension. He said that if I were disinterested on my own account, I had no right to be for Mme Levasseur and her daughter, and that . . . I should solicit it and obtain it at any price" (O.c., I, 381).

Diderot, in undertaking to exonerate Seneca before those who accused him of greed and cynicism, was equally defending his own compromises with society and condemning the absolutism of his former friend. Rousseau had spent the last decade of his life in a mounting campaign of self-justification. From the *Confessions* he had gone on to the dialogue *Jean-Jacques juge de lui-même*, and nearing the end of his days, he stationed himself on a Paris street corner, distributing a pamphlet called "A Tout Français aimant encore la justice et la vérité" to those passersby whose countenances seemed to promise impartiality. He was, at last, convinced that he was the only human being left on earth, the rest being automatons. Diderot looked back upon his blind infatuation with Rousseau, calling it "the passion of his youth." He described how they had become united by "a secret instinct of kinship," and how he had shared all of Rousseau's tastes and eccentricities. In retrospect, he wondered: "What happened to that manner of existence, so whole, so violent, so sweet? I scarcely remember it; personal interest slowly weakened it. I am old, and I confess, not without bitterness and regret, that at an advanced age one has the bonds of habit; but there remains in us, at our side, only the vain shadow of friendship. Ah! Friends! Friends! There is one, count firmly only on him. It is he whose benevolence and charity you have long experienced, who has done you so many good and bad turns. You will survive all the others, this one will abandon you only when you die: it is you, try to be your own best friend" (*A.-T.*, III, 204).

Diderot recalled the time of his friendship with Rousseau, when he had written the condemnation of Seneca appearing in his translation of Shaftesbury's *Inquiry concerning Virtue and Merit*. Now the mature philosopher saw the author who had accused Seneca of greed and cowardice as "a child, a scatterbrain, in whom unfortunately a certain talent for writing had preceded common sense" (*A.-T.*, III, 178). Diderot added a note in which he linked his injustice toward Seneca with his passion for Rousseau:

While I made common cause with the wicked to denigrate a virtuous philosopher, I allied myself with fools to put a hypocrite on a pedestal. I remained the stubborn defender of the latter against enlightened friends, who warned me about the consequences of a dangerous intimacy. Their prediction was not long in being realized. Alas! It was in the midst of an intoxication which I cherished that I saw, with as much grief as surprise, that for many long years what I had pressed against my bosom was a monster. (A.-T., III, 178–79, Note 2)

Diderot remembered himself at thirty as a self-infatuated young man, who, like Rousseau, had entertained the most extravagant notions of his own value while cavalierly denouncing better men than he as worthless. He saw the negative side of youthful idealism in its unwillingness to consider life according to realistic standards, its refusal to recognize the good that often coexists with the morally reprehensible. The dream of an unblemished world, which Rouseau carried with him to the grave, did not demonstrate the superior virtue of the dreamer at all. Rather, it revealed his egotistical desire to preserve his own self-esteem, even at the cost of damning the rest of humanity. Diderot admonished his younger self for daring to attack Seneca: "You judge the man by a fantastic model about which experience with the world and your own danger will soon disabuse you. When you have come to grips with yourself and have known the agony of the sage, you will be sorry for the atrocious insults you addressed to Seneca" (A.-T., III, 177).

The man who refused to admit his own motives, withdrawing from civilization in order to cherish a picture of himself as good and others as wicked, turns the natural narcissism of the young into a middle-aged perversion. To say anything useful to humanity, to do anything of value for it, one must first comprehend its real nature, and the best way to gain this understanding is by the assiduous examination of the self: "He who studies himself will be well advanced in the knowledge of others, if, as I believe, there is no virtue unknown to the wicked, nor vice alien to the good" (*A.-T.*, III, 173).

Seneca had remained at Nero's side during the period of the Emperor's worst excesses. Compared with Imperial Rome, the Paris of Louis XV was positively edifying, and in showing Seneca as the man who had done the right thing by holding fast to his duties in the face of incredible difficulty, Diderot accomplished his own apology as well. In analyzing Seneca's dilemma, Diderot presented the most extreme example of the problem of the relationship between the philosopher and the world. Seneca was, by overwhelming agreement, both a fine man and an eloquent and austere philosopher; Nero, on the other hand, was the ultimate embodiment of despotism and depravity. That Seneca failed either to reform Nero or to strengthen the moral fiber of Roman society was not, to Diderot's mind, a relevant issue. Such a task lay beyond the capacity of the man who was neither divine nor considered himself to be. Seneca was merely human, and for Diderot he was to be judged precisely by what he did in a concrete, historical situation, offering at best limited opportunities for constructive action.

Thus the last days of the philosopher were spent in weighing his first days. The essay on Seneca redressed the wrongs that Diderot believed he had committed in his headstrong youth when he damned a philosopher who had decided to live in the world, and praised one who set himself above mankind. In assuming the responsibilities of a family, Diderot had wed his fate to that of his society, as Seneca had. The man who courted the Neckers to gain advantages for his son-in-law and enjoyed the favors of Catherine the Great was a long way from Diogenes, motioning to Alexander to move out of his light. He was thoroughly enmeshed in the machinery of a dozen relationships; obligations to his wife, his child, his mistress, and his friends held him firmly within a compromised world. But these ties were of his own making; they were the natural results of his needs. Diderot believed that others, as well as himself, were to be judged by their actions within the context of a realistic view of man and society, not by some chimera of absolute virtue concocted in hermetic solitude. Rousseau had denied the existence of evil within himself, and died terrified of a universal conspiracy. The wickedness he repudiated came back in the form of a malignant cosmos, threatening his very sanity. His last years were spent passing back and forth from the euphoria of the chosen to the agonies of the damned.

The end of Diderot's life was neither ecstatic nor desperate. He had shucked off his illusions of himself as "a man of the most perfect probity," recognizing the penchant for small cruelties which had initiated so many of his acts. He had jettisoned, one after another, the exalted passions he had once felt for Rousseau, for Sophie, even for Grimm. As his vision and hearing failed, he began to think of casting off even his body. "The heavy baggage will be moving on," he told his sister when his teeth began to loosen. "I see these preparations for the great voyage being made without caring much" (*C.*, XV, 126).

Diderot died on July 31, 1784, in an elegant new house on the Rue Richelieu which Grimm had arranged for Catherine of Russia to provide. He might have been amused by the spectacle of his devout wife and his rich son-in-law persuading the reluctant priest of Saint-Roche to allow the *philosophe* a splendid religious funeral.

Notes

1 / Probity without Religion

1. Jean Starobinski, *Jean Jacques Rousseau, la transparence et l'obstacle* (Paris: Plon, 1958).

2. Rousseau described his perception of himself as unchanging in a passage from *Rousseau juge de Jean-Jacques:* "He is what nature made him: education has modified him but little. If his faculties and strength had suddenly developed from birth, he would have been about what he was in his maturity, and now after sixty years of pain and misery, time, adversity, and men have still changed him very little. Until the end of his life he will not cease to be an aged child." *Œuvres complètes* (Paris: Bibliothèque de la Pléiade, 1959), I, 799–800.

3. In Lester Crocker, ed., *Anthologie de la littérature française du XVIIIe siècle* (New York: Holt, Rinehart & Winston, 1972), p. 51.

4. Voltaire, *Œuvres* (Paris: Lefevre, 1829), XXXVII, 334.

5. Montesquieu, *Œuvres complètes* (Paris: Bibliothèque de la Pléiade, 1951), p. 714.

6. Robert Mauzi, *L'Idée du bonheur dans la littérature et la pensée françaises au XVIIIe siècle* (Paris: Armand Colin, 1960), p. 590.

7. "Everything which favors society is ornamented with the names just, equitable, etc., everything which offends its interests is called

unjust." Julien de La Mettrie, *Textes choisis* (Paris: Editions sociales, 1954), p. 54.

"True virtues are those which add to the public felicity and without which society cannot subsist." Helvétius, *De l'esprit* (London, 1781), p. 160; see also p. 131.

"Virtue is only the art of being happy oneself for the felicity of others," Paul Henri Dietrich d'Holbach, *Système de la nature* (Hildesheim: Georg Olms Verlagsbuchhandlung, 1966), p. 450.

8. In his celebrated study of the eighteenth century's attitudes toward society, Carl Becker makes the point that theological concepts were frequently to be found in laicized form behind the proposals for a more rational order. *The Heavenly City of the Eighteenth-Century Philosophers* (New Haven: Yale University Press, 1932).

9. *Essai sur le mérite et la vertu* (trans., Diderot), *A.-T.*, I, 79.

10. J.-J. Rousseau, *Du Contrat social . . . Discours sur l'origine de l'inégalité* (Paris: Classiques Garnier, 1954), p. 66.

11. Marquis de Sade, *Œuvres complètes* (Paris: Au Cercle du livre précieux, 1966), III, 470, 437.

12. In Crocker, *op. cit.*, p. 733.

13. See Jean Fabre, "Deux Frères ennemis: Diderot et Jean-Jacques," *D.S.* 3.

14. Arthur Wilson provides an excellent description of Diderot's family background and early years. See in his definitive biography *Diderot* (New York: Oxford University Press, 1972), Chap. I. See also: Viscount John Morley, *Diderot and the Encyclopaedists, Works* (London: Macmillan, 1921), XI; Massiet du Biest, *La Fille de Diderot* (Tours: chez l'auteur, 1949); Lester Crocker, *The Embattled Philosopher* (East Lansing: Michigan State College Press, 1954); André Billy, *Diderot* (Paris: Les Editions de France, 1932); Jean Pommier, *Diderot avant Vincennes* (Paris: Boivin, 1939); and Franco Venturi, *La Jeunesse de Diderot* (Paris: Skira, 1939).

15. On the occasion of Diderot's bicentenary, François Helme published an appreciation of the philosopher's relationship to the medical profession, linking his interest to his father's métier. "Diderot dans notre art," *La Presse médicale*, no. 89 (Paris, 1913).

16. "Mémoires pour servir à l'histoire de la vie et des ouvrages de Diderot," *A.-T.*, I, xxx–xxxi.

17. Rousseau recounts his adventures in the first five books of the *Confessions*, *O.c.*, I.

18. *O.c.*, I, 348. William Blanchard makes the point that Rousseau's intense feelings for Diderot in prison were the product of his tendency toward immediate and overwhelming identification with the persecuted. See his psychological study *Rousseau and the Spirit of Revolt* (Ann Arbor: University of Michigan Press, 1967), pp. 52–53.

19. Jean Catrysse, *Diderot et la mystification* (Paris: Nizet, 1970), p. 22.

20. It should be noted, however, that Rousseau later attributed his taste for "persiflage" to his friend rather than to any natural bent of his own in that direction. "As for Diderot, I do not know why all my conversations with him tended to make me more satirical and mordant than my nature impelled me to be." *O.c.*, I, 405n.

21. In their notes to the Pléiade edition of his works, Gagnebin, Osmont, and Raymond discuss the problem of Rousseau's children and the various arguments which have been put forward concerning their abandonment. *O.c.*, I, 1416–22.

22. *O.c.*, I, 347. See also Fabre, *op. cit.*

23. "Sur les femmes," *A.-T.*, II, 252. See Henri Lefebvre, *Diderot* (Paris: Les Editeurs réunis, 1949), p. 218.

24. For an amusing description of Diderot's labors to accommodate his parsimonious wife and his extravagant mistress, see Chaps. 4 and 5 of André Billy, *Diderot* (Paris: Editions de France, 1932). See also Wilson's account of his relationship with Mme de Puisieux in *Diderot*, pp. 64–66.

25. See René P. Legros, "Diderot et Shaftesbury," *MLR*, 19 (1924).

26. But the weight of Shaftesbury's argument is precisely the contrary: religion and virtue are separable in both senses. The devout are not necessarily moral and the atheist is not perforce wicked. Among other insults, Diderot would seem to believe his brother incapable of catching the drift of Shaftesbury's thesis.

27. Venturi analyzes the favorable critical reaction to Diderot's translation of Shaftesbury in the *Journal de Trévoux,* the *Journal des Savants,* and especially that of Desfontaines in his *Jugements sur quelques livres nouveaux. Op. cit.,* pp. 68–70.

28. Crocker remarks that the title "seemed to purport a reflection of Voltaire's famous *Philosophic Letters* and a rebuttal of Pascal's *Thoughts.*" *The Embattled Philosopher,* p. 68.

29. *Lettres de M. de Marville,* ed. A. de Baslisle (Paris: Champion, 1896), I, x.

30. *Ibid.,* p. xxii.

2 / Philosophy and Power

1. Louis XV offered Rousseau a pension for his *Devin du village,* but Rousseau, terrified at the prospect of being presented at court, refused it. He commented in the *Confessions:* "In receiving this pension all I needed to do was flatter or be still: yet who was assuring me it would be paid? So many steps to take, so many people to solicit! It would have cost me more disagreeable worries to keep it than to get along without it." *O.c.,* I, 380.

For an account of Rousseau's dealings with King George III see Lester Crocker, *Jean-Jacques Rousseau, The Prophetic Voice* (New York: Macmillan, 1973), II, Chap. 8. William H. Blanchard discusses the significance of Rousseau's attempts to provide legislation for Poland and Corsica in *Rousseau and the Spirit of Revolt* (Ann Arbor: University of Michigan Press, 1967), Chap. 13.

2. For an account of the honors heaped upon Grimm by his patrons, see André Cazes, *Grimm et les Encyclopédistes* (Paris: Les Presses universitaires de France, 1933), Chap. IX.

3. For a valuable synthesis of the attraction exerted by French philosophical ideas on the sovereigns of Europe in the latter decades of the eighteenth century see John G. Gagliardo, *Enlightened Despotism* (New York: Crowell, 1967).

4. Sebastien Mercier, *Tableau de Paris* (Amsterdam, 1783–89), IV, 160.

5. Jacques Proust, *Diderot et "l'Encyclopédie"* (Paris: Armand Colin, 1962), p. 175.

6. In the words of Massiet du Biest, " 'Boutique' was an invention of Diderot, comparing his worktable, his books and his manuscripts to his father's cutlery shop!" Massiet du Biest, *La Fille de Diderot* (Tours: chez l'auteur, 1949), p. 29.

7. *A.-T.*, XVI, 161–62. As Michel Butor remarked, "We can regard the whole *Encyclopédie* as a gigantic mystification of which the controllers were the agents, an entirely useful mystification, but during the course of which the moments of heroism and fright must have been compensated for by some remarkable laughs." "Diderot le fataliste et ses maîtres," *Critique*, no. 228 (May 1966), 230.

8. *Textes choisis de l'Encyclopédie* (Paris: Editions sociales, 1962), p. 187.

9. Diderot also described the necessity for cunning in ferreting out the secrets of mechanical processes to be described in the *Encyclopédie*: "There are circumstances where the artists are so impenetrable that the shortest way would be to enter into apprenticeship oneself. There are few secrets which one would not eventually learn by this means, one should divulge all these secrets without exception." *A.-T.*, XIV, 492.

10. Quoted by Cazes, *op. cit.*, p. 45.

11. Proust comments on Grimm's treatment of the *Encyclopédie* in the *Correspondance littéraire*: "Everything was done so that the enemies of the *Encyclopédie* seemed negligible dust, and so that the dictionary took on the size and the weight of a monumental work, become the affair of a whole people." *Op. cit.*, p. 66.

12. Palissot (de Montenoy) Charles, *Œuvres* (Liège: Plomteux, 1777), II, 103.

13. *Ibid.*, 105.

14. Moreau, *Mémoire pour servir à l'histoire des Cacouacs* (Geneva: Slatkine Reprints, 1968), p. 56.

15. For a discussion of the fortunes of Diderot's play see Wilson, *Diderot* (New York: Oxford University Press, 1972), pp. 271–74.

16. Cited by René Pomeau, intro. to *Julie ou la Nouvelle Héloïse* (Paris: Garnier Frères, 1960), p. viii.

17. See Proust, *op. cit.*, pp. 98–116 for a detailed account of the crisis of 1758.

18. *Du Contrat social* . . . (Paris: Classiques Garnier, 1954), p. 201, *n.* 1.

19. J. Pappas and G. Roth, "Les 'Tablettes' de Diderot," *D.S.* 3, 309.

20. André Billy raised the question in his biography of the philosopher: "An idea often occurs to me when I think of this mysterious Sophie Volland and I am astonished to see her, at forty-three, so harshly treated by her mother. I say to myself that perhaps she was not having her first adventure, that she must have had some grave sin of her youth to expiate. That would explain many things, first that she was not married. If I am wrong, may her ghost forgive me!" *Diderot* (Paris, Editions de France, 1932), p. 272.

21. For an interesting résumé of the little which is known of Sophie Volland, see Wilson, *Diderot*, pp. 228–31. See also Lydia-Claude Hartman, "A Propos de Sophie Volland," *D.S.* 12, for a perceptive analysis of the philosopher's relationship with Sophie.

22. For a detailed account of the way in which the estate was divided, see Proust, *op. cit.*, Chap. III.

3 / Bad Times

1. See Arthur Wilson, *Diderot* (New York: Oxford University Press, 1972), p. 366.

2. *C.*, III, 226. The logic of this idea is similar to Rousseau's when he rejected Voltaire's argument against the existence of a benevolent providence not because it was unconvincing but because it made him feel bad: "Instead of the consolation I was hoping for, you only [afflict] me; one would say that you fear lest I fail to see how unhappy I am." *O.c.*, IV, 1060.

3. It was of utmost importance to all the freethinkers, not just Diderot, that their lives should appear blameless to compensate for the daring of their opinions. As Leland Thielemann remarked, "One of Hobbes's most important legacies to the philosophers of the French Enlightenment was to remain the example of his life, to which they could point with family pride as incontrovertible evidence 'that unbelievers could live as uprightly as the faithful.'" "Diderot and Hobbes," *D.S.* 2, 222.

4. For a thorough treatment of the complex history of this work, see Georges May, *Diderot et "La Religieuse"* (New Haven: Yale University Press, 1954).

5. For a description of Diderot's state of mind at this juncture, see the chapter on "Diderot pessimiste: La Crise de mélancholie des années 1760–1762," in Georges May, *Quatre Visages de Diderot* (Paris: Hatier-Boivin, 1951).

6. Diderot apparently composed *Le Neveu de Rameau* in 1761 but continued revising it until as late as 1772. (See Paul Vernière's notice in the *Œuvres romanesques*, p. 874.) The text was first published by Goethe, in a German translation of a manuscript copy which has since disappeared. Various manuscripts turned up in the nineteenth century, but it was not until 1890 that Georges Monual, librarian of the Comédie-Française, chanced upon a copy in Diderot's own handwriting in a bookdealer's stall.

7. See Jean Seznec, *Essais sur Diderot et l'antiquité* (London: Oxford University Press, 1957), Chap. I: "Le Socrate imaginaire." See also Raymond Trousson, *Socrate devant Voltaire, Diderot et Rousseau: la Conscience en face du mythe* (Paris: Lettres modernes, 1967).

8. See Joseph Waldauer, "Society and the Creative Man in Diderot's Thought" (subsection "Diogenes and Aristippus in Diderot's Thought"), *D.S.* 5, for a discussion of his attitude toward the Stoical and Cynical positions.

4 / The Project of Sincerity

1. Diderot's article on "Hobbism" appeared in the eighth volume of the *Encyclopédie* in 1765, the same year that d'Holbach brought the *Treatise of Human Nature* to his attention. Leland Thielemann concludes that while Diderot was greatly taken with much of Hobbes's thinking, he ultimately found the English philosopher excessively pessimistic. See "Diderot and Hobbes," *D.S.* 2. See also Diderot's letter to Naigeon (*C.*, XII, 45) for his reaction to d'Holbach's translations of Hobbes.

2. In his chapter "Diderot sexologue," Georges May discussed Diderot's vocation as an amateur doctor. *Diderot et "La Religieuse"*

(New Haven: Yale University Press, 1954), pp. 98–114. See also the study by Dr. Cabanès, "Diderot et les sciences médicales," *Médecins amateurs* (Paris: Albin Michel, 1932), pp. 157–96.

3. Georges Daniel discusses the curious rapport which existed between the personalities of the participants in the dialogue and the subject of their conversation in "Le Rêve de d'Alembert," *D.S.* 12.

4. Jean Starobinski puts great emphasis on his subject's desire to be completely and instantaneously comprehended, his emotions felt, expressed, and understood without the cumbersome intermediary of language to introduce ambiguity. See *Jean-Jacques Rousseau, la transparence et l'obstacle* (Paris: Plon, 1958).

5. Yvon Belaval provides a most helpful schema of the argument of the *Paradoxe sur le comédien* as well as an analysis of its significance in *L'Esthétique sans paradoxe de Diderot* (Paris: Gallimard, 1950), Part III, Chap. 2.

6. Robert Lewinter offers the following definition of Diderot's mature concept of the "sage": "The sage according to Diderot differs from the sage of the Stoics. His perfection does not reside in a haughty and egocentric development of the ego but in an individual and social development, essentially allocentric. The sage transcends society, but in order to serve it better." "L'Exaltation de la vertu dans le théâtre de Diderot," *D.S.* 8, 160.

5 / Adviser to the Empress

1. For example, see Lester Crocker, *The Embattled Philosopher* (East Lansing: Michigan State College Press, 1954), p. 379.

2. Maurice Tourneux, *Diderot et Catherine II* (Paris: Calmann Lévy, 1899), p. 82; quotations from Diderot, cited on pp. 445, 242, 109. For an account of the peculiar fortunes of the manuscript in Russia, where it was all but inaccessible until 1952, see P. Vernière's introduction to *Mémoires pour Catherine II* (Paris: Garnier, 1966).

3. Jean Guéhenno describes the affair in *Jean-Jacques, Histoire d'une conscience* (Paris: Gallimard, 1962), II, Chap. 6.

4. For a discussion of the relationship between these works, see Robert Niklaus, "Diderot's Moral Tales," *D.S.* 8; also, Herbert

Dieckmann's introduction to Diderot, *Contes* (London: University of London Press, 1963).

5. *Du Contrat social . . . Discours sur l'origine de l'inégalité* (Paris: Classiques Garnier, 1954), p. 40.

6. "The males and the females united fortuitously, according to chance, occasion, and desire, without the word being the interpreter of what they had to say to each other: they parted with the same facility." *Ibid.*, p. 52.

7. *O.p.*, p. 509. Although on the whole population in Western Europe increased during the eighteenth century, the peculiar patterns of famine, plague, and migrations were frequently perceived as a sign that the world was running down, its fertility somehow exhausting itself. Montesquieu concluded in the *Esprit des lois* that "Europe today is still in need of laws which favor the propagation of the human species: thus, while Greek politicians always tell us of the large number of citizens who work the republic, modern politicians only speak to us of means for increasing that number." *Œuvres complètes* (Paris: Bibliothèque de la Pléiade, 1951), p. 710. In the *Lettres persanes* (Paris: Garnier-Flammarion, 1964), he attributes the fact that "the earth is less populated today than it was before" to two causes among the Christian nations: the interdiction of divorce and the institution of religious celibacy (pp. 183, 185–89). Thus the Enlightenment argument against these two Catholic beliefs was from the beginning utilitarian. Diderot was echoing the century's conviction that a healthy society must expand its numbers when he advocated liberal divorce laws and inveighed against celibacy. See also his advice to Catherine of Russia concerning these subjects. Tourneux, *op. cit.*, pp. 196–99.

For a description of demographic trends in France, see Olwen H. Hutton, "Life and Death among the Very Poor," in *The Eighteenth Century*, ed. Alfred Cobban (New York: McGraw-Hill, 1969).

8. See Paul Vernière's discussion in his introduction to the dialogue. *O.p.*, 519–23.

6 / The Trickster's Turn

1. Albert Camus, in *L'Homme révolté* (Paris: Gallimard, 1951), p.

322, describes the very program for the novelist which Diderot, almost two centuries before, dismissed as unworthy: "Beings always escape us and we escape them too: they lack firm contours. Life, from this point of view, has no style. It is only movement which chases after form without ever finding it. Man, torn in this way, searches in vain for that form which would give him the limits between which he would be King.

"What is the novel, in effect, but that universe where action finds its form, where the words at the end are spoken, being rendered to being, where each life assumes the face of destiny. The fictional world is but the correction of this world, following man's profound wish. The novel fabricates destiny on command."

2. Otis E. Fellows points out the fallacy of considering the novel a straightforward defense of the belief in determinism. See "*Jacques le fataliste* Revisited," in *From Voltaire to La Nouvelle Critique* (Geneva: Droz, 1970), p. 98.

3. See Lester Crocker, "*Jacques le fataliste*, une expérience morale," *D.S.* 3.

7 / The Final Accounting

1. Bossuet, "Méditations sur l'Evangile," *Œuvres posthumes* (Paris, 1731), I, 5. See also *Système de la nature* (Hildesheim: Georg Olms Verlagsbuchhandlung, 1966), p. 436.

2. This letter, which is published without date or address by G. Roth and J. Varloot in the "complement" to Diderot's *Correspondance* (XVI) appears to me to have been written around 1772 to Mme de Maux, the woman with whom Diderot enjoyed a bittersweet love affair, presumably his last. I make this assumption because of the rather blunt, world-weary tone of the letter, which frequently characterized his correspondence with her, as contrasted with the kind of affectionate deference he expressed when writing to Sophie.

3. Rousseau read parts of his work to select audiences at the home of the Marquis de Pezay, the poet Dorat, and the Prince of Sweden, beginning in December 1770. It is likely that Diderot received fairly detailed accounts of these readings, since they occasioned

considerable scandal. In May 1771 Mme d'Epinay requested that the Chief of Police, M. de Sartine, dissuade Rousseau from continuing, because she and her friends were depicted in an unfavorable light. See the notes of Gagnebin, Osmont, and Raymond to the *Confessions. O.c.,* I, 1613.

4. For an illucidating account of how the Préface-Annexe came to be part of *La Religieuse,* see Herbert Dieckmann, "The *Préface-Annexe* of *La Religieuse," D.S.* 2.

5. Quoted by Georges May in *Diderot et "La Religieuse"* (New Haven: Yale University Press, 1954), p. 27. See also Dieckmann, *op. cit.,* pp. 21–22.

6. See Douglas A. Bonneville, *Diderot's "Vie de Sénèque"* (Gainesville: University of Florida Press, 1966), p. 7, for an account of the order of these editions.

List of Works Cited

Becker, Carl. *The Heavenly City of the Eighteenth-Century Philosophers.* New Haven: Yale University Press, 1932.

Belaval, Yvon. *L'Esthétique sans paradoxe de Diderot.* Paris: Gallimard, 1950.

Billy, André. *Diderot.* Paris: Les Editions de France, 1932.

Blanchard, William H. *Rousseau and the Spirit of Revolt.* Ann Arbor: University of Michigan Press, 1967.

Bonneville, Douglas. *Diderot's "Vie de Sénèque."* Gainesville: University of Florida Press, 1966.

Butor, Michel. "Diderot le fataliste et ses maîtres." *Critique,* no. 228 (May 1966).

Cabar. 's, Dr. "Diderot et les sciences médicales." *Médecins amateurs.* Paris: Albin Michel, 1932.

Camus, Albert. *L'Homme révolté.* Paris: Gallimard, 1951. Eng. trans., *The Rebel.* New York: Knopf, 1954.

Catrysse, Jean. *Diderot et la mystification.* Paris: Nizet, 1970.

Cazes, André. *Grimm et les Encyclopédistes.* Paris: Les Presses universitaires de France, 1933.

Cioranescu, Alexandre. *Bibliographie de la littérature française du XVIIIᵉ siècle.* 3 vols. Paris: Centre national de la recherche scientifique, 1969.

Crocker, Lester, ed. *Anthologie de la littérature française du XVIIIe siècle*. New York: Holt, Rinehart & Winston, 1972.

———. *The Embattled Philosopher. A Biography of Denis Diderot.* East Lansing: Michigan State College Press, 1954.

———. *"Jacques le fataliste,* une expérience morale." *D.S.* 3.

Daniel, Georges. "Le Rêve de d'Alembert." *D.S.* 12.

Dieckmann, Herbert. *"The* 'Préface-Annexe' *of* 'La Religieuse.' " *D.S.* 2.

Diderot, Denis. *Mémoires pour Catherine II.* Ed. Paul Vernière. Paris: Garnier Frères, 1966.

Fabre, Jean. "Deux Frères ennemis: Diderot et Jean-Jacques." *D.S.* 3.

Fellows, Otis E. *From Voltaire to La Nouvelle Critique.* Geneva: Droz, 1971.

Gagliardo, John G. *Enlightened Despotism.* New York: Crowell, 1967.

Guéhenno, Jean. *Jean-Jacques, Histoire d'une conscience.* Paris: Gallimard, 1962.

Hartman, Lydia-Claude. "A Propos de Sophie Volland." *D.S.* 12.

Helme, François. "Diderot dans notre art," in *La Presse médicale,* no. 89 (Paris, 1913).

Helvétius, Claude A. "De l'esprit": or *Essays on the Mind and Its Several Faculties.* London, 1781.

Holbach, Paul Thiry, Baron d'. *Système de la nature.* Hildesheim: Georg Olms Verlagsbuchhandlung, 1966.

Hutton, Olwen. "Life and Death among the Very Poor," in *The Eighteenth Century.* Ed. Alfred Cobban. New York: McGraw-Hill, 1969.

La Mettrie, Julien de. *Textes choisis.* Paris: Editions sociales, 1954.

Lefebvre, Henri. *Diderot.* Paris: Les Editeurs réunis, 1949.

Legros, René P. "Diderot et Shaftesbury." *MLR,* 19 (1924).

Lettres de M. de Marville, Vol. I., ed. A. de Boislisle. Paris: Champion, 1896.

Leutrat, Jean-Louis. "Autour de la genèse du *Neveu de Rameau,"* in *Revue d'Histoire littéraire de la France,* May–August 1968.

Lewinter, Robert. "L'Exaltation de la vertu dans le théâtre de Diderot." *D.S.* 8.

Massiet du Biest, Jean. *La Fille de Diderot*. Tours: chez l'auteur, 1949.

Mauzi, Robert. *L'Idée du bonheur dans la littérature et la pensée françaises au XVIIIe siècle*. Paris: Armand Colin, 1960.

May, Georges. *Diderot et "La Religieuse."* New Haven: Yale University Press, 1954.

——. *Quatre Visages de Diderot*. Paris: Hatier-Boivin, 1951.

——. "Le Dix-huitième siècle à l'honneur: Bilan d'un effort de dix-sept ans." *D.S.* 14.

Mercier, Sébastien. *Tableau de Paris*, Vol. IV. Amsterdam, 1783–89.

Montesquieu, Charles S. *Œuvres complètes*. Paris: Bibliothèque de la Pléiade, 1958.

——. *Lettres persanes*. Paris: Garnier-Flammarion, 1964.

Moreau, J. B. *Mémoire pour servir a l'histoire des Cacouacs*. Geneva: Slatkine Reprints, 1968.

Morley, John (Viscount). *Diderot and the Encyclopaedists*, *Works*, Vol. XI. London: Macmillan, 1921.

Mornet, Daniel. *Diderot, l'homme et l'œuvre*. Paris: Boivin, 1941.

Niklaus, Robert. "Diderot's Moral Tales." *D.S.* 8.

Palissot (de Montenoy), Charles. *Œuvres*, Vol. II. Liège: Plomteux, 1777.

Pappas, J. and Roth, G. "Les 'Tablettes' de Diderot," *D.S.* 3.

Pommier, Jean. *Diderot avant Vincennes*. Paris: Boivin, 1939.

Proust, Jacques. *Diderot et "l'Encyclopédie."* Paris: Armand Colin, 1962.

Rousseau, Jean-Jacques. *Du Contrat social . . . Discours sur l'origine de l'inégalité*. Paris: Classiques Garnier, 1954.

Sade, Marquis de. *Œuvres complètes*, Vol. III. Paris: Au Cercle du livre précieux, 1966.

Seznec, Jean. *Essais sur Diderot et l'antiquité*. London: Oxford University Press, 1957.

Starobinski, Jean. *Jean-Jacques Rousseau, la transparence et l'obstacle*. Paris: Plon, 1958.

Thielemann, Leland. "Diderot and Hobbes," *D.S.* 2.

Tourneux, Maurice. *Diderot et Catherine*. Paris: Calmann Lévy, 1899.

Trousson, Raymond. *Socrate devant Voltaire, Diderot et Rousseau: la Conscience en face du mythe.* Paris: Lettres modernes, 1967.

Vandeul, Marie-Angélique (née Diderot). *Mémoires pour servir a l'histoire de la vie et des ouvrages de Diderot.* A.-T., I.

Varloot, Jean. *Diderot, textes choisis.* Paris: Editions sociales, 1952.

Venturi, Franco. *La Jeunesse de Diderot.* Paris: Skira, 1939.

Voltaire. *Œuvres,* Vol. XXXVII. Paris: Lefevre, 1829.

Waldauer, Joseph. "Society and the Creative Man in Diderot's Thought." *D.S.* 5.

Wilson, Arthur. *Diderot.* New York: Oxford University Press, 1972.

A Brief List of Other Works in English

On the Enlightenment and the Encyclopédie

Cobban, Alfred. *A History of Modern France*, Vol. 1, 1715–1799. New York: Braziller, 1965.

Gay, Peter. *The Enlightenment: An Interpretation*. New York: Knopf, 1966.

Lough, John. *Essays on the "Encyclopédie" of Diderot and d'Alembert*. London: Oxford University Press, 1968.

Niklaus, Robert, Ed. P. E. Charvet. *A Literary History of France* Vol. 3. *The Eighteenth Century (1715–1789)*. London: Fox & MacFarlane, 1970.

Williams, E. N. *The Ancien Régime in Europe: Government and Society in the Major States, 1648–1789*. New York: Harper and Row, 1970.

Diderot

Josephs, Herbert. *Diderot's Dialogue of Gesture and Language: "Le Neveu de Rameau."* Columbus: Ohio State University Press, 1969.

Loy, J. Robert. *Diderot's Determined Fatalist*. New York: Columbia University Press, 1950.

O'Gorman, Donal. *Diderot the Satirist: "Le Neveu de Rameau" and*

Related Works, an Analysis. Toronto: University of Toronto Press, 1971.

Rousseau

Cassirer, Ernst. Ed. and Trans., Peter Gay. *The Question of Jean-Jacques Rousseau.* New York: Peter Smith, 1954.

Cobban, Alfred. *Rousseau and the Modern State.* London: 1934. 2d ed., The Shoestring Press, 1964.

Crocker, Lester. *Jean-Jacques Rousseau: The Quest (1712–1758).* New York: Macmillan, 1968.

———. *Jean-Jacques Rousseau: The Prophetic Voice (1758–1778).* New York: Macmillan, 1973.

D'Alembert

Grimsley, Ronald. *Jean D'Alembert, 1717–83.* London: Oxford University Press, 1963.

Hankins, Thomas. *Jean D'Alembert: Science and the Enlightenment.* New York: Oxford University Press, 1970.

Index